Buddhism and Friendship

Buddhism and Friendship

Subhuti (with Subhamati)

WINDHORSE PUBLICATIONS

Also by Subhuti and available from Windhorse Publications:
Bringing Buddhism to the West
Sangharakshita: A New Voice in the Buddhist Tradition
The Buddhist Vision

Published by Windhorse Publications
11 Park Road
Birmingham
B13 8AB
email: info@windhorsepublications.com
web: www.windhorsepublications.com

Cover design by Marlene Eltschig
Cover photo Corbis
Printed on acid-free paper by Interprint Ltd, Marsa, Malta

British Library Cataloguing in Publication Data:
A catalogue record for this book is available from the British Library

ISBN   1 899579 62 1

Contents

Part Two: The Meaning of Spiritual Friendship

Part Three: Spiritual Friendship in Practice

About the Authors

Subhuti was born Alex Kennedy, in Chatham, England, in 1947. He joined the Western Buddhist Order (WBO) in 1973 and has since devoted himself to the practice and teaching of Buddhism. He played a part in establishing both the London Buddhist Centre and a retreat centre in Spain, and also developed a training process to prepare men to join the WBO.

Since 2000, Subhuti has been Chairman of the College of Public Preceptors, to which the founder of the WBO, Sangharakshita, handed on his responsibilities on his retirement. Currently based in Birmingham, England, Subhuti spends part of each year in India, leading retreats and giving lectures. He has written five other books.

Subhamati was born Malcolm Holmes in Newport, South Wales, in 1953. He worked as a university administrator in London until becoming involved in Buddhism. Ordained by Subhuti in 1990, he subsequently taught for several years at the Croydon Buddhist Centre, and now works as an assistant to Subhuti.

Preface

This book is for anyone interested in Buddhism or friendship, or in the relation that those two topics might have to each other.

Readers won't need a great deal of prior knowledge of Buddhism. Anyone who has digested one of the many general introductions now available should be able to understand me without too much difficulty. But in addition to those still relatively new to Buddhism, I would like my ideas on spiritual friendship to reach practising Buddhists of all kinds. Although they might not all agree with me on every point, I hope they will find something here to enrich their own understanding and practice of the Dharma. Indeed, I hope that people practising in other spiritual traditions will find something of benefit in what I have to say on the role of friendship in the spiritual life.

Although the book is for the general reader, it draws from a wide variety of scriptural and literary sources, and some readers may want to follow up my references. I have therefore provided numbered endnotes, but the non-scholar, who just wants to find out what I have to say, can feel free to ignore them.

1

As far as possible, I try to avoid burdening readers with foreign words. However, there are some Buddhist concepts for which, in my opinion, no truly satisfactory English word is available. For that reason, I make extensive use of two or three Sanskrit terms. It seems better to 'naturalize' these words than translate them with a cumbersome phrase or a succinct but misleading approximation. Each such term is explained when it first appears in the text. My choice of Sanskrit in these cases reflects my sources. However, the same principle of consistency with sources leads me to use Pali when I am discussing teachings or stories drawn from the Pali scriptures (e.g. Sāriputta, not Śāriputra). Only in one instance do I depart from this principle: although the relevant sources are mainly Pali, I use the Sanskrit word for friendship (*mitratā*) rather than the similar Pali form (*mittatā*). In this case, I prefer the Sanskrit form for the sake of consistency with usage in my other books and those of my teacher Sangharakshita.

It seems fitting that a book about friendship should itself be the product of a friendship. The book has its origins in a series of talks that I gave some years ago. However, my friend Subhamati has rewritten that material, expanding Part One and integrating into each chapter some of my more recent thinking on the subject.

Both of us would like to express our thanks to four fellow members of the Western Buddhist Order who improved the book by reading and commenting on the first version: Dhammadinna, Kulananda, Nagabodhi, and Vishvapani. Since then, Jnanasiddhi of Windhorse Publications has given us advice that has helped us to improve the text still further.

As always, I also have to thank Sangharakshita, who founded our order and initiated the emphasis on spiritual friendship that is one of its distinguishing features. Most of what I have to say on the subject derives ultimately from him.

Part One

Friendship Past and Present

Introduction

The Whole of the Spiritual Life

In one of the many Buddhist scriptures is an intriguing account of a conversation between the Buddha and a monk called Ānanda. This monk was the Buddha's younger cousin, and the two had known one another since Ānanda's boyhood. Ordained about two years after the Buddha's enlightenment, Ānanda remained close to him from that time onwards. In fact, during the last twenty-five years of the Buddha's life, Ānanda served him as a personal attendant, taking the opportunity to store his teacher's words in his memory in order to pass them on to future generations. The two men seem to have been good friends.

The scripture starts with Ānanda approaching the Buddha, intent on sharing a thought. After saluting his teacher and sitting down, he enthusiastically declares his insight into the importance of spiritual friendship. Something – perhaps the cumulative effects of his daily association with the Buddha – has suddenly made him realize how crucial it is to his progress. Risking a bold assertion, Ānanda declares that spiritual friendship is no less than half of the spiritual life.

But he has not quite got it right. The Buddha immediately corrects him: spiritual friendship is the *whole*, not the half, of the spiritual life.[1]

This discourse will be familiar to those well versed in the scriptures of the Theravāda school of Buddhism, but many other Buddhists may be quite unaware of it. It is rarely mentioned in the now vast body of secondary works about Buddhism in English. Yet the message is clear and important: the Buddha himself said that spiritual friendship is *the whole* of the spiritual life. Anyone who is a Buddhist, or is interested in Buddhism, therefore has a good reason to take the idea seriously.

Admittedly, for many people, Eastern or Western, the thought that spiritual friendship is in some sense the totality of Buddhism will seem strange. Many of them will already have some idea or image that sums up what it means, or might mean, to be a Buddhist. The idea of the cessation of pain, for example, or freedom from the repeated cycle of birth and death, is a key notion for some. Others might see in their mind's eye a path, perhaps leading ahead through a forest or upwards to a high place. For others, the thought of meditation may encapsulate the essence of Buddhism, bringing with it a picture of someone sitting poised and serene, eyes half closed. But in such images as these, Buddhists see themselves as essentially alone, rather than with friends.

Alternatively, inspired by a different Buddhist tradition, some people might imagine the ideal Buddhist as active in relation to others, like a hero rescuing children who are thoughtlessly playing in a burning house, or a doctor working tirelessly to save lives amid an epidemic. In images of this kind, Buddhism appears as something one does for others, without necessarily getting close to them personally.

Such images are valid and beautiful symbols of what we do when we practise the *Dharma*, the Buddha's teaching. They are all drawn from the Dharma itself, and most are important for one or other of the various Asian Buddhist traditions. However, no traditional school, as far as I am aware, leads us to an understanding of Buddhism in terms of friendship, even though this too is part of the teaching. Perhaps the time for this particular key to the Dharma has not come until now.

Some readers may sense some mismatch between their existing notion of Buddhism and the idea that friendship is integral to it. After all, isn't Buddhism the religion that urges us to 'wander solitary as a rhinoceros's horn'? Doesn't it constantly warn us of the dangers of 'attachment'? Don't some Tibetan Buddhists seal themselves up in caves for years to avoid human contact? None of that sounds particularly friendly.

Before embracing the idea of Buddhism as a path of friendship, we will want to ask some questions. The most obvious one is 'in what sense can spiritual friendship be described as *the whole of the spiritual life*?' Presumably the meaning can't be quite literal, as that would exclude such things as ethics, meditation, or study, which are normally considered part of the Buddhist way, but are not intrinsic to our common-sense idea of friendship. Then, where – apart from in this one scripture I have mentioned – is the evidence to support the claim that friendship is an important part of Buddhism? If it is true, why do so many Buddhist books fail to mention it?

And what exactly does 'spiritual friendship' mean? Does it really refer to anything other than a spiritual 'teacher–student relationship', about which (perhaps) we know quite a lot already? And even in that case, isn't the word 'friendship' more metaphorical than literal? After all, many Buddhists do not think of their teacher as a 'friend' in the ordinary sense of the word, but rather as a revered benefactor, with whom they would not presume to claim personal intimacy. If the teacher–student relationship does not exhaust the meaning of 'spiritual friendship', what other sorts of relationship does the concept include?

Those already actively involved in the practice of the Dharma will have more questions. They will be curious to know what difference the Buddha's words about spiritual friendship should make to their practice. Indeed, how can friendship fit in with the notion of *practice* at all? Isn't friendship something that just happens spontaneously, and therefore something that cannot easily be assimilated to the concept of practice, with its connotations of system and discipline?

These are valid and important questions – ones that I have reflected on a good deal – and in the following pages I want to attempt some answers.

In the first part of the book, my aim is to anchor the theme of spiritual friendship in Buddhist scriptures. Buddhism emphasizes the possibility – indeed the necessity – of direct personal experience of the spiritual realities with which it is concerned, and therefore it does not rely on its canonical texts in quite the same way that some religions do. Nevertheless, an attempt to show that spiritual friendship is part of Buddhism can hardly ignore those texts. As I will show in the first three chapters of Part One, the references to friendship in the Buddhist canon, while not particularly numerous, are certainly weighty and significant, and support the idea that the Buddha saw spiritual friendship as crucially important.

But that fact inevitably poses a further question: given that the scriptural basis for the importance of friendship is strong, why hasn't the theme been very prominent in Buddhist discourse through the intervening ages? Or to put it another way, why is it only very recently – and in the West – that some of us have felt the need to pick up the theme of friendship from the Buddhist scriptures? The answer to this question is most likely to be found by examining the social conditions under which we are trying to practise the Dharma in the West today (conditions that are now being replicated in the East). What is it about our culture that has impelled some of us to make friendship conscious to a degree that doesn't seem to have been necessary before? I examine this question in Chapter 4.

Part Two of the book is more philosophical in nature. It articulates my attempt to understand clearly and fully what spiritual friendship actually is. The scriptures – while offering some suggestive indications – don't give any systematic answer to that question. If I am right in thinking that Buddhists today can benefit from cultivating friendship, such a 'theory' of friendship may be useful in helping us to understand exactly what we are trying to cultivate.

In addition to a theory, people who want to develop spiritual friendship will need practical guidance. In the third and final Part, I suggest some principles and precepts I think will be useful to all those who want to turn spiritual friendship from an ideal into a lived experience.

As you will gather from this outline, this book is not a memoir of my personal experience of spiritual friendship. We already have a good book of that kind: Maitreyabandhu has filled the niche admirably with his *Thicker than Blood: Friendship on the Buddhist Path*. My purpose here is different from his: to put the case for the role of friendship in Buddhism, and to show rather more systematically what Buddhist friendship means in principle and in practice. Accordingly, although I include a few anecdotes, I focus on scriptural sources, on ideas and argument, and on practical precepts, rather than on personal reminiscence.

Nevertheless, the book is firmly rooted in my personal experience. Indeed, it is my heartfelt wish, in writing about spiritual friendship, to share with others something that has enriched beyond measure my own life as a Buddhist. I want to communicate the importance of spiritual friendship, to suggest what it can mean and where it can lead – things I know at first hand. I hope my words will feed the flame of spiritual friendship among Buddhists of all kinds, and that some of the warmth of that flame will pass into the wider world.

1
The Liberation of the Heart
Friendship and the Path

Kalyāṇa mitratā

The Buddha told Ānanda that spiritual friendship was the whole of the spiritual life. But how well does this English phrase 'spiritual friendship' convey what they actually had in mind?

We can't be sure what language Ānanda and the Buddha were speaking, but in Sanskrit – which may not be too remote from it – the words I am translating as 'spiritual friendship' are *kalyāṇa mitratā*.[2] As we will see, there are scriptures that say or show important things about friendship without ever mentioning *kalyāṇa mitratā*. Nevertheless these two words sum up the theme of this book, and will reappear frequently, so before we get under way it is worth pausing to take a close look at their meaning.

Mitratā is quite simple: it means 'friendship', and is derived from the word for 'friend': *mitra*. *Kalyāṇa* is not so straightforward. According to a standard dictionary, it has various meanings: 'beautiful, charming, auspicious, helpful, morally good'.[3] In translations of Buddhist scriptures, you may also see *kalyāṇa* rendered as 'lovely' or 'noble'. This range of meaning may seem puzzlingly wide, but the underlying sense fuses the ideas of goodness and beauty, implying that what is good *is* beautiful. Occasionally in the scriptures, *kalyāṇa* literally means 'beautiful', as in *kalyāṇa dassana* (nice looking), but it usually refers to a spiritual beauty that pleases the heart and mind rather than the senses. According to a well-known formula that recurs in several places, the Dharma itself is 'kalyāṇa in its beginning, kalyāṇa in its middle, and kalyāṇa in its ending' – good and beautiful through and through, one might say.[4]

A friendship that is kalyāṇa is therefore 'lovely' not just because it is pleasant or warm, but because it is based on a shared orientation to what is ultimately beautiful: the transcendental reality known to the enlightened mind. Likewise, a kalyāṇa mitra is a 'good friend', not only in the sense of someone known intimately and trusted without reservation, but, more fundamentally, a friend who is a good person, endowed with beautiful ethical and spiritual qualities.

Clearly, the various meanings of 'kalyāṇa' allow for several possible ways of translating 'kalyāṇa mitratā' into English. Some translators offer 'good friendship', others 'lovely friendship' and so on. No English translation can capture all the nuances perfectly, but I generally prefer the phrase 'spiritual friendship' because it allows us to keep in view the main thing that distinguishes this kind of friendship from others: its roots in shared spiritual aspirations and experiences.

In the first widely available English versions of the Pali scriptures, 'kalyāṇa mitratā' was rendered (in some contexts, though not in others) as 'friendship with what is lovely' – suggesting that the term meant no more than a sort of abstract affinity for goodness, rather than a human relationship. However, a more recent translation rejects this 'impersonal' interpretation of 'kalyāṇa mitratā' (which, the translator suggests, was an error rooted in a misreading of Pali grammar) and restores the personal meaning that has always been accepted as the right one for most contexts. (Readers who would like to explore this rather technical question will find a fuller discussion in the Appendix.)

Ānanda surprises himself by coming to the conclusion that kalyāṇa mitratā is no less than half of the spiritual life. The Buddha replies that this is still an underestimate: it is not the half but the whole of it.

'The spiritual life' means the way of life that leads to enlightenment, the path taught by the Buddha.[5] The Buddhist scriptures describe this path in many different ways, sometimes in outline and sometimes in detail, sometimes from one viewpoint, sometimes another. Probably the best known of these descriptions is the noble eightfold path. So it comes as no surprise that the Buddha, in trying to explain *why* spiritual friendship is the whole of the spiritual life, tells Ānanda,

> When a bhikkhu [monk] *has a good friend, a good companion, a good comrade, it is to be expected that he will develop and cultivate the Noble Eightfold Path.*[6]

To emphasize the point, the Buddha goes on to say that such a monk develops each of the eight aspects of that path, namely, right view, right intention, right speech, right action, right livelihood, right effort, right awareness, and right meditation.

You might wonder whether the Buddha, in describing spiritual friendship as 'the whole of the spiritual life', was indulging in a little poetic embellishment, or perhaps exaggerating the point in order to impress it upon Ānanda (who could sometimes be a little slow on the uptake). But apparently this was not the case, for the Buddha made exactly the same high claim for spiritual friendship to other people on at least two occasions. On one of these, Sāriputta, his leading disciple, approached him and asserted that kalyāṇa mitratā was the whole of the spiritual life. The Buddha approved this view with the words, 'Good, good,

Sāriputta!' and went on to explain the matter in the same way as to Ānanda.[7]

The commentary on these scriptures (which, though only written down about a thousand years later, seems to represent an oral tradition stretching back to the Buddha's time) explains that Sāriputta, being a more advanced disciple than Ānanda, had correctly judged the importance of kalyāṇa mitratā, whereas Ānanda had not. Ānanda had seen that a disciple's progress on the path stemmed from the combination of individual effort and the benefits of friendship. He had therefore attributed to each of these two factors an equal and distinct role. In other words, from Ānanda's viewpoint, a spiritual life deprived of kalyāṇa mitratā would still be, in a manner of speaking, half a spiritual life – which is presumably better than none.

Sāriputta, however, penetrating more deeply, had reached the same insight as the Buddha himself. He had seen that, while kalyāṇa mitratā and individual effort both contribute to the spiritual life, they don't do so by supplying two separate portions of that life. According to the commentary, any attempt to apportion the 'credits' for one's spiritual progress between oneself and one's spiritual friends is like trying to work out which characteristics a child has inherited from the mother and which from the father. You can never do it with any exactitude because a human being is a whole in which the features inherited from each parent merge seamlessly with one another.[8] Similarly, with regard to the noble eightfold path, it is impossible to say, for example, that individual effort produces right view, while kalyāṇa mitratā produces right intention, and so on. The spiritual path arises – not only in its general outline, but also in each and every particular – through the synthesis of personal striving and friendship.

Of course, applying the logic of the commentary the other way round, we could legitimately reverse the Buddha's dictum and say that individual effort is the whole of the spiritual life.

However, the Buddha did not say that, perhaps because he had already made the need to strive so clear on other occasions.

In the third scripture that includes this teaching, we find the Buddha conversing with King Pasenadi of Kosala, one of his lay disciples. The king reveals to the Buddha his dawning realization that the Dharma 'is for one with good friends, good companions, good comrades, not for one with bad friends, bad companions, bad comrades'. The Buddha remarks, 'So it is, great king!' – and then gives Pasenadi a full account of his earlier conversation with Ānanda, adding, 'Therefore, great king, you should train yourself thus: "I will be one who has good friends, good companions, good comrades."'[9] The fact that the Buddha spoke of kalyāṇa mitratā in exactly the same way to monks and lay disciples underscores the universality of this teaching, which belongs not just to a monastic or a lay lifestyle, but to the spiritual life in its widest or most fundamental sense.

On each of the three occasions, the Buddha says that, in addition to its relevance to the noble eightfold path, there is also a second sense in which spiritual friendship is the whole of the spiritual life: it is through relying on him, the Buddha, as a good friend, that beings caught in the suffering of the cycles of birth and death may be set free. In this additional explanation, the meaning of 'friend' seems more like 'benefactor'. There is nothing to surprise us here, as we are already familiar with the idea of the Buddha as a benefactor of humanity. But in the Buddha's first explanation of his meaning, 'friendship' seems to carry its normal, literal sense of a mutually loving relationship. The idea that Buddhist spiritual life somehow comprises or requires this kind of relationship is less familiar to us, and calls for exploration.

Our starting point is the idea, stated in each of the three scriptures, that 'it is to be expected' that when a spiritual aspirant has 'a good friend, a good companion, a good comrade', he or she will 'develop and cultivate the Noble Eightfold Path'. But why is it to be expected? We could easily speculate on the answer, but

15

how did the Buddha himself see it? He doesn't enlarge on the point in these three texts, but fortunately there is another story from the scriptures that casts light upon it.

Meghiya and the mango grove

This story concerns the Buddha and a monk called Meghiya, who (like Ānanda later on) served the Buddha as a personal atten-dant.[10] The Buddha and Meghiya are staying alone together in a secluded rural spot. One day, while returning after seeking alms in a nearby village, Meghiya notices a beautiful mango grove near the banks of the river. It strikes him as an idyllic setting for medi-tation, and he is seized by a keen desire to go there and strive for spiritual attainment. On getting back to the Buddha, he immedi-ately asks permission to meditate in solitude in the mango grove. The Buddha mildly points out that in doing so Meghiya would leave him alone (a tactful reminder to Meghiya of his duty as an attendant), and suggests that he wait a while until some other monk might join them.

Meghiya, however, is full of impatience for what he could achieve in the grove, and repeats his request. To strengthen his hand, he points out that the Buddha (being the Buddha) has nothing further to achieve, while he, Meghiya, still has a lot of spiritual work to do. The Buddha once more declines, for the same reason, but Meghiya presses his request yet again, stressing his wish to strive in meditation.

In the Buddhist scriptures, the act of putting a request three times, ignoring all signs of reluctance, expresses a tough determi-nation to get what one wants, come what may. Not only that, but Meghiya's comparison of himself with the Buddha is as if to say, 'Well, *you're* all right, aren't you? *You* don't need anything!' He is, in effect, putting his request in such a way that the Buddha cannot refuse. The Buddha, seeing that Meghiya is not open to persuasion, can only comment, 'Well, Meghiya, if you speak of striving, what can I say? Do as you think best.'

Meghiya duly takes his leave and spends the afternoon in the mango grove. However, things don't work out as he hoped. Instead of soaring into higher realms of consciousness, his mind is overcome by lustful daydreams and malicious fantasies. He is left helplessly marvelling at the lowness of his thoughts: 'I've gone forth from worldly life, inspired by faith. I've become a monk. Yet here I am, overwhelmed by unwholesome mental states!'

We aren't told how long Meghiya has been a disciple of the Buddha, but he doesn't seem to be very experienced. Newcomers to meditation are often buoyed up by optimism gained from early success, and may blithely assume that a smooth ascent lies ahead, but more often than not they are disappointed. Even after setting up ideal conditions, like Meghiya's mango grove, one is likely to collide sooner or later with an invisible wall of unconscious resistance. Such humiliations can be valuable lessons, but it is easy to get disheartened by them if one is practising alone.

Fortunately, Meghiya has a friend. Chastened, he returns to the Buddha, and admits what has happened. The Buddha does not rebuke him, but sees that the time is ripe to enlarge his understanding.

The Buddha starts by explaining that when a disciple has not yet reached the spiritual maturity required for the liberation of the heart, five things are necessary. The first is kalyāṇa mitratā:

> When liberation of heart is not fully mature, Meghiya, five things conduce to full maturity. What five?
>
> In this connection, Meghiya, a monk is one with a lovely friend, one with a lovely companion, one with a lovely intimate [or good friends, good associates, good companions]. When liberation of the heart is not fully mature, Meghiya, this is the first thing that conduces to full maturity.[11]

Interestingly, the Buddha does not say that the first thing a disciple needs is a teacher. In other words, he doesn't seem to see formal instruction as the essence of the relationship he has in mind. The text unequivocally speaks of a *friend*, using two synonyms ('companion' and 'intimate') to underline the point.[12] The question of what exactly 'friendship' means belongs to a later part of this book, but for now we can assume that the Buddha must have meant relationships that are personal, warm, and familiar.[13]

The second thing that leads to the liberation of the heart is that the disciple should be virtuous, living in accordance with the ethical precepts. Thirdly, he needs to have easy access to talk that conduces to the spiritual life in all its aspects. Fourthly, his energy should constantly be roused for the spiritual life. (In other words, he needs inspiration and encouragement.) Finally, he must develop wisdom.

The order in which the Buddha mentions the five conditions is not random. Like many lists in the Buddhist scriptures, this is a progressive sequence. In fact, the sequence maps essentially the same process of spiritual evolution as the eightfold path: a journey beginning with moral discipline, progressing through spiritual effort, and arriving at liberating understanding. But it does so from a new viewpoint – one that highlights spiritual friendship. It is crucial to notice that, although the sequence is progressive, kalyāṇa mitratā is not left behind when one progresses to the second condition (virtue). Far from it: the Buddha emphasizes that if you have the benefit of kalyāṇa mitratā, it is likely that you will acquire each of the other four things in turn:

> *This, Meghiya, may be looked forward to by the monk who is one with a lovely friend, one with a lovely companion, one with a lovely intimate – that he will become one possessing morality [virtue]....*
>
> *That such talk as ... conduces to ... superknowledge, to awakening ... he will gain at will ... without trouble....*
>
> *That he will dwell as one with energy initiated with the purpose of abandoning unskilled states, with the purpose of under-*

taking skilled states....

> *that he will become one possessing insight [wisdom] ... that is*
> *... penetrative, properly leading to the destruction of [suffering].*[4]

In other words, although the five conditions are a progressive series, they are not like five sections of a straight line. Kalyāṇa mitratā is not only the first condition, but also a precondition for each of the remaining four. Spiritual friendship is what gets the spiritual life going effectively to begin with, and what sustains it later on.

Having explained the five conditions in this way, the Buddha adds that, once a monk is established in all five, he should then undertake a range of meditation practices that will act as antidotes to mental hindrances of the kind that over-whelmed Meghiya in the mango grove.

As in his conversation with Ānanda, the essence of the Buddha's message to Meghiya is that it is to be expected that a disciple who has spiritual friendship will progress on the spiritual path. But this time, the logic of the expectation is easier to infer – partly because the Buddha has reformulated the path in terms of kalyāṇa mitratā, and partly because the story itself casts light on his meaning.

The five conditions

Firstly, Meghiya needs to learn the importance of friendship: he has been in the company of the Buddha, but has not fully bene-fited from it, because he has not yet learned how to be a friend. He is thinking only of himself, and doesn't seem to have much sense of what a rare and delightful opportunity it is to be the compan-ion of an enlightened being.

Secondly, there is *virtue*. Virtue does not mean just abstain-ing from doing bad. According to a famous verse in the *Dhammapada*, the Buddha teaches us not only to 'refrain from

19

evil', but also to 'practise the good' (and finally 'purify the mind'). Meghiya is not a bad man, but he is not quite as good as he thinks he is. His eagerness to get to that mango grove, despite the Buddha's gentle attempt to dissuade him, suggests selfishness and the absence of a sense of duty: he is, after all, supposed to be the Buddha's attendant. Aside from the question of formal duty, his action shows a lack of gratitude to a generous friend.

Close friendship with good people is the most effective way to make one's own conscience more delicate, in the same way that your health tends to improve if you move to where the air is cleaner. By contact with kind, generous, honest friends, we come to understand – and to feel – what goodness really is. This is because the sources of good and evil are human emotions, and our emotional life is shaped more through contact with other people than through moral theories or teachings. Ideas are not enough to check unwholesome desires, which in the long run can only be resisted by an opposite emotional force. According to Buddhist psychology, there are two positive emotions that allow us to overcome an impulse to do something wrong. One is *shame*. This is the uncomfortable feeling that we get when we fall short of our own ethical standards – a healthy emotion, not to be confused with irrational guilt or timid inhibition. The other is known (in Sanskrit) as *apatrāpya* – for which, unfortunately, there is no English equivalent.[15] It is sometimes translated with phrases like 'fear of blame by the wise', but this is misleading, making it sound like a cowed dread of scolding. *Apatrāpya* is really our sense of the viewpoint of friends we look up to. It flows from our appreciation of their goodness, not from fear. When we feel an impulse to do something wrong, it makes us see how that action would look in the eyes of our good friends, and so holds us back from it.[16]

Shame is an inner ethical compass and its accuracy depends on one's spiritual maturity. At first, it is not a very delicate or precise instrument: it only offers a rough guide. But through close association with spiritual friends we can strengthen and refine our moral awareness by means of *apatrāpya*. This is why it is to be expected that one who has the benefit of kalyāṇa mitratā will also acquire virtue. Meghiya, for instance, clearly needs to spend more time in the company of spiritual friends, absorbing a sense of how they think and feel, before he will be ready to go it alone.

The third condition listed by the Buddha as necessary for the maturing of the heart's liberation is easy access to talk that conduces to the spiritual life. If we have no friends who share our interest in the Dharma, our understanding of it is likely to develop slowly and perhaps lopsidedly, affected by the subjective biases that we inevitably bring to it. We need people with whom we can chew over what we have heard or read, and explore what it all means in practice – people who share our enthusiasm, and with whom we can relax and speak freely.

The Buddha gives Meghiya examples of appropriate subjects for such talk, all of them central themes of the Dharma: letting go of worldly desires, a simple lifestyle, ethical behaviour, meditation, and so on. He specifies not only the topics but also the spirit of the talk: it should be 'suited to the opening up (or uncovering) of the heart'.[17] In other words, one has to apply the Dharma directly to oneself, especially to one's inner life of mental states, in order to purify that life. This kind of talk is not theoretical debate, but personal communication – an honest meeting of minds and hearts. It is likely to include an element of confession (which would flow naturally from the preceding condition, virtue). Such talk develops gradually, on the basis of trust and intimacy. We are most likely to find it with close spiritual friends.

Meghiya has not yet experienced enough of this kind of talk. In his experiment with solitary meditation in the mango grove, unwholesome mental states overwhelm him, taking him by surprise and leaving him baffled and mortified. We see that as yet he has uncovered little of his own heart.

An interest may grow into an enthusiasm when fed by encouragement and example, as a fire blazes up when it has fuel and air. This brings us to the fourth condition – the rousing of energy (*viriya*). Our spiritual friends stir up our love and admiration. The more time we spend with them, the more we feel inspired to become like them.

Viriya is not just 'energy' but 'energy in pursuit of the good'.[18] It is a spiritual vigour that is heroic but refined: heroic because it relishes a difficult challenge, refined because it has to work with the subtlest of materials – the mind itself. *Viriya* is the kind of energy needed for the transformation of one's inner world through meditation and mindfulness. This kind of energy doesn't come easily. It has to be learned. Those drawn to the spiritual life are often, at the outset, impelled by quite different forces: naive idealism perhaps, or psychological pain, or a fascination for what seems strange and remote. These motives have to be transformed before one can make much progress. *Viriya* cannot be taught, but it can be *caught* from those who already have it. However, the transmission is slow, requiring the prolonged and repeated contact that we find only in friendship.

Finally, we come to *wisdom* – the fifth condition for the maturing of the heart's liberation. In Buddhism, 'wisdom' is a deep intuitive awareness of reality. It means seeing through the fundamental illusions of human life: the illusion, for example, that we live in a world of distinct and substantial objects, and that some of these objects can be possessed and so give us security or lasting satisfaction; or the illusion that each of us has an eternal, unchanging soul or self, like a rocky island standing firm in the stormy sea of existence. Wisdom – the force that shatters these illusions – lies at the heart of the Buddha's enlightenment. It was probably wisdom that Meghiya hoped to attain in the mango grove.

But reading or hearing such definitions of wisdom doesn't make anyone wise. That was Meghiya's fundamental mistake. He must already have known something about the Dharma before he went to the mango grove, and this 'something' probably included some of the ideas included in the last four conditions. Having received the instruction manual, he thought he was ready to set up shop on his own. What he hadn't grasped was the importance of kalyāṇa mitratā.

Today we can find Buddhist teachings in abundance in books or download them from the Internet. But has this proliferation of words produced a proliferation of wisdom in the world? Words can set us facing in the right direction, but cannot, on their own, bring us to the experience they refer to. Wisdom is developed not by hearing or reading alone, but by the spiritual life in its wholeness – a wholeness that, as we have seen, the Buddha chose to define in terms of spiritual friendship.

The best way to get a foretaste of wisdom is through direct contact with the wise. When we meet them, though, we should not expect to see wisdom written on their faces. We have to catch at least a glimpse of their inner life, and even share that life to some degree. The most natural and effective way to do that is through friendship with them. Wisdom sometimes emerges from spiritual friendship very directly: the scriptures contain stories in which a disciple's 'Dharma eye' opens in the course of a conversation with the Buddha. But even for those who make the breakthrough in other situations – in meditation, for instance – some experience of spiritual friendship is almost always a precondition.

The womb of enlightenment

We shouldn't be too hard on Meghiya: his aspiration may have been rather naive, but it was genuine. As things turned out, he faced up to his mistake honestly, and received a valuable lesson. The essence of that lesson is that spiritual friendship is a kind of womb or matrix from which all aspects of the spiritual life – even wisdom – emerge. It is not something we leave behind after our spiritual apprenticeship. The qualities, attitudes, habits, and skills that we need to attain enlightenment will appear gradually and progressively within the medium of kalyāṇa mitratā, like crystals forming in a solution. This is the basic sense in which kalyāṇa mitratā is 'the whole of the spiritual life'. As we will see later, however, even this is not the whole story.

It follows that those who want to develop spiritually should make spiritual friendship a priority. It is not that spiritual practice is impossible or fruitless until one has spiritual friends, but it does seem that isolated practice is a kind of preliminary, the fruits of which can only fully mature when one finds kalyāṇa mitratā. No doubt there are gifted individuals who make major spiritual breakthroughs on their own, with little or no assistance from friends, but such individuals are the exceptions rather than the rule. In fact, if one takes the Buddhist teaching of rebirth into account, their capacity to go it alone might not be what it seems: we can't know what benefits of spiritual friendship they enjoyed in previous lives.

The discourse on the five conditions was especially appropriate to Meghiya as an antidote to his individualism, but that does not mean that it is *only* valid for Meghiya, or for one type of personality alone. This is shown by the fact that the same teaching reappears elsewhere. In another scripture, the Buddha teaches his monks what to say if anyone asks them what conditions lead to enlightenment.[19] The detailed reply that he recommends is the same, word for word, as his teaching to Meghiya. Once again, kalyāṇa mitratā is not only the first condition, but also the basis for each of the remaining four.

Perhaps the teaching began as a response to the needs of one individual, but the Buddha must have seen that it had a universal aspect. Meghiya did not see the value of friendship until it was pointed out to him, and many others might make the same mistake.

2
One in Mind

Friendship as the Goal

Vertical and horizontal friendship

In the story of Meghiya, we see his selfishness and naivety contrasted with the Buddha's tactful wisdom. In that sense, the friendship we are shown is unequal, for one of the partners is spiritually much more advanced than the other. This is an important kind of spiritual friendship, but not the only one.

The Pali Text Society's *Pali-English Dictionary* offers two definitions of *kalyāṇa mitra* (or rather, of its Pali equivalent, *kalyāṇa mitta*).[20] The first one is 'a good companion, a virtuous friend, an honest, pure friend'. Such a friend is said to 'have faith, be virtuous, learned, liberal and wise'. In this broad sense, *kalyāṇa mitra* is the opposite of *pāpa mitra* ('evil friend'). Inequality, if it is implied at all, is not central to this meaning.

In the second sense, a *kalyāṇa mitra* is 'a spiritual guide, a spiritual adviser'. In this case, there clearly *is* an unequal or hierarchical aspect to the relationship: a guide must be someone whose spiritual knowledge and experience are superior to one's own (why else accept him or her as a guide?) However, this second meaning is to be understood as a special variation of the first. (The dictionary classifies it as a technical term.) In other words, the role of spiritual guide belongs in the context of friendship.

If you are lucky, you may find a friend whom you recognize as much more spiritually mature than you are – someone who arouses your faith by displaying insight and compassion that greatly exceed your own. Such a friend may become your teacher, but that is not quite the point: he or she may transform your life by example, rather than by teaching. We could call this kind of relationship 'vertical', as it takes place between people on different levels of development.

But there is also a kind of friendship that exists between those who are approximately on the same level. These friends are like spiritual brothers or sisters, or, if you prefer, fellow wayfarers. Although friends of this kind are more easily found than guides, they too are very precious. The spiritual path is long, arduous, and easily lost. Our guide, if we are lucky enough to have one, is likely to have many other claims on his or her attention, and won't always be at hand to resolve our doubts, revive our flagging spirits, or steer us past the byways that tempt our erring feet. It is important to have not just a guide but also companions on the path. Such companions represent the 'horizontal' dimension of spiritual friendship.

Perhaps in passing I should make it clear that my desire to speak of teacher–student relationships in the context of friendship is not meant to devalue the experience of those who feel a different kind of connection with their spiritual teacher. Some Buddhists would say that their teacher – with whom their personal contact may have been quite limited – is their 'friend' in the sense of 'kind benefactor' rather than in any sense that implies personal intimacy. While respecting such experiences, I know that the teacher–student relationship *can* be a form of friendship, and that this too can be profoundly transforming.

The distinction between vertical and horizontal is real and useful, but it is also flexible: there is no sharply drawn boundary between the two categories. The spiritual path is an infinitely graded continuum, so it is not always easy to discern which of two people is further ahead. It would be better to say that there is one kind of spiritual friendship, which has vertical and horizontal dimensions. Some friendships may be obviously positioned on one axis, but in other cases you might at different times experience vertical and horizontal aspects in one and the same relationship.

Some readers may doubt whether the horizontal axis of spiritual friendship really is found in Buddhism, for many Buddhists have come to understand *kalyāṇa mitratā* only in its second, narrower sense. But in fact it was originally understood to include not only teacher–disciple relationships but also any friendship between good people who revere the Buddha and his Dharma. This emerges clearly from, for example, the Buddha's teaching to the lay disciple Dīghajānu:

> *And what is good friendship [kalyāṇa mitratā]? Here ... in whatever village or town a family man dwells, he associates with householders or their sons, whether young or old, who are of mature virtue, accomplished in faith, virtue, generosity and wisdom; he converses with them and engages in discussions with them. He emulates them in regard to their accomplishment in faith, virtue, generosity and wisdom. This is called good friendship.*[21]

Although these words were spoken to a layman, we should not conclude that horizontal friendship was only relevant to lay disciples. One could ask for no better example of it than the friendship between Sāriputta and Moggallāna, who were foremost among the Buddha's monks. Sāriputta was known as the *senāpati*, the 'marshal' of the Dharma, and was famed for his wisdom, while Moggallāna was more renowned for psychic powers attained through meditation. Despite these differences of emphasis, the two seem to have been fairly evenly matched as regards their overall spiritual attainments.

Long before they ever met the Buddha, Sāriputta and Moggallāna were already firm friends, and as young men they went out into the world together in search of enlightenment. They promised to share with one another whatever fruits their spiritual quest produced, making a pact that if one of them 'found the Deathless' he would inform the other. At first, knowing nothing of the Buddha, they became followers of another ascetic. But one day, Sāriputta happened to meet Assaji, a disciple of the Buddha. The two got into conversation, and Assaji briefly explained the essence of the Dharma, as far as he himself had grasped it. Immediately on hearing Assaji's words, wisdom arose in Sāriputta's mind. Realizing that he had obtained the aim of their mutual quest, he promptly set off, faithful to his vow, to tell his friend.

At his approach, Moggallāna saw instantly (before Sāriputta had even spoken) that Sāriputta had found the Deathless. They now felt sure who their real teacher was, even though they had not yet seen him face to face. They immediately sought out the Buddha and took ordination from him.[22] In a very short time, they both progressed to complete enlightenment.

Interestingly, their names continue to appear in connection with each other in the scriptures after their enlightenment. One tale in particular leaps out of the often dry Pali texts with a touching and amusing picture of their friendship.[23] The two were meditating in the open air one night. Sāriputta had recently shaved his head and it was shining in the light of the full moon. As they sat peacefully, two *yakkhas* (demons) happened to fly past, and Sāriputta's head, gleaming in the darkness, caught their eye. Unable to resist the temptation, one of the yakkhas mischievously gave Sāriputta a great clout on the head. (The yakkha, by the way, suffered immediate and dire karmic retribution for this action, but we won't go into that aspect of the story.) Moggallāna, being gifted with psychic powers, could perceive spirits and so witnessed the whole affair. Sāriputta had not seen the demons, nor did he seem to feel the blow: deeply absorbed in his meditation, he sat on undisturbed.

Out of concern for his friend, Moggallāna approached him and asked, 'Are you all right?' Sāriputta replied, 'I'm fine, although I do seem to have a slight headache.' Moggallāna, lost in admiration, exclaimed, 'How wonderful, Sāriputta! What extraordinary power! You can meditate so profoundly that you don't even notice a blow on the head from a yakkha – a blow that could have felled an elephant, or shattered a mountain peak.' Sāriputta replied immediately, 'How wonderful! What extraordinary power *you* have, Moggallāna: you can actually *see* a yakkha, whereas I can't even see a mud-sprite.'

We need not feel obliged to take the supernatural aspect of the story literally, but the meaning of the tale is clear enough. One thing it illustrates is the Buddhist custom of rejoicing in merits: Moggallāna marvels at the depth of Sāriputta's meditation; Sāriputta praises Moggallāna's psychic power. We glimpse a characteristic of their friendship – a delighted appreciation of one another's qualities. The contrast between those qualities shows that while the two are friends and equals, they are not duplicates. Their spiritual attainments manifest differently – Sāriputta's in a deep, inward stillness, Moggallāna's in the acute perception of hidden worlds. It seems that, contrary to what you might guess, the spiritual development of friends is not a convergence upon the same bland anonymity: increasing selflessness leads to no loss of individuality.

But for me, the most interesting aspect of this story is simply that it shows that Sāriputta and Moggallāna remained close friends after their enlightenment. Just the fact that they often chose to stay together, meditate together, and not to dwell constantly in solitude, bears witness to this.

Sāriputta and Moggallāna were *arahants* – that is, they were fully enlightened. They had nothing more to achieve, nothing to learn or gain from friendship with one another, or with anyone. As arahants, they were liberated from all desire to cling to anything in the world, feeling no attachment whatever to things or people. Despite this inner freedom, it seems that the flame of their friendship burned as brightly as ever. This is worth reflecting on. It means we can only understand their friendship as an expression of their enlightened state, for in them nothing unenlightened remained to be expressed.

The Pali text of the yakkha story does not mention kalyāṇa mitratā as such, but if the relationship between Sāriputta and Moggallāna is not spiritual friendship, what are we to call it? And in a way, the tale reveals a deeper aspect of kalyāṇa mitratā than the one revealed in Meghiya's story. In that case, spiritual friendship was treated as a means to an end: it was presented as a kind of path leading to the goal of the liberation of the heart. In the story of Sāriputta, Moggallāna, and the yakkhas, however, spiritual friendship is shown as an aspect of the end itself – that is, as one dimension of enlightenment.

It seems that friendship belongs not only to the path but also to the goal of the spiritual life, or to put it another way, the path and the goal merge with one another, and spiritual friendship is woven into the fabric of both. It is important to grasp this point, because when we understand spiritual friendship only in terms of the path, we are in danger of cultivating friendship not for itself, but 'for the sake of my spiritual development'. Thinking in this way, we could end up by treating our friends as 'equipment' in the service of our own spiritual ambitions, in which case they wouldn't really be friends at all. We can only experience genuine spiritual friendship when we see it as an end in itself, or at least as an intrinsic part of some larger end. Otherwise, we reduce it to something resembling the conventional type of friendship that is based on mutual usefulness (a distinction I will explore fully in Chapter 5).

The vision of friendship as part of the goal is expressed more fully in another *sutta* (or 'discourse'), which tells the moving story of Anuruddha and his friends.

Three enlightened friends

Anuruddha, Nandiya, and Kimbila are staying together in a quiet forest grove, where the Buddha goes to visit them one evening, after emerging from solitary meditation. On becoming aware of their teacher's arrival, the three monks hasten to welcome him, one relieving him of his bowl and outer robe, another making a seat ready, the third bringing water to bathe his feet. When they are all seated, the Buddha first checks that they are in good health and adequately supplied with food. He then begins to ask them about their way of life together. His first question is, in essence, whether they get on well with one another. Anuruddha confirms that he and the other two are 'living in concord, with mutual appreciation, without disputing, blending like milk and water, viewing each other with kindly eyes.'[24]

The Buddha (who knows very well that not all his monks get along so cordially) enquires *how* they manage to do so. Anuruddha explains that he considers himself fortunate to be living the spiritual life together with such companions as Nandiya and Kimbila. To do so is, in his opinion, a 'great gain' for him. The way they live together is an expression of *mettā*, that is, of loving-kindness or friendliness. Accordingly, he maintains a positive attitude towards the other two in every possible way – kindly deeds, affectionate speech, and loving thoughts. Anuruddha's words suggest that he has been developing mettā towards his companions as a practice, something nurtured through mindfulness, a conscious part of the spiritual life.

However, what began as a practice has now become second nature. He has reached the point of routinely putting the others' desires before his own. He simply asks himself, 'Why should I not set aside what I wish to do, and do what the others wish to do?' And then he does precisely that. In conclusion, he tells the Buddha, 'We are different in body, venerable sir, but one in mind.'

Nandiya and Kimbila, for their part, reply to the Buddha in the same way, each saying that he has surrendered his own inclinations and is living according to the will of the other two. They all agree that they are 'different in body, but one in mind'.

As they have *all* given up their wills to each other, there is no question of one dominating the other two, or being the leader. (Anuruddha is simply their main spokesman, probably through having been ordained longest.) Their unanimous self-abnegation presents us with a mystery: how can they act at all, if none of the three 'wills'? A will must be operative among them, for they have not frozen into immobility. Whose will is it, then? It seems that they experience a shared will, or rather a mysterious coincidence of wills, based on deep mutual awareness and harmony.

The Buddha expresses pleasure at their words and goes on to ask whether they are living 'diligent, ardent, and resolute'. In other words, are they striving for spiritual progress? Anuruddha confirms that they are. Again, the Buddha asks *how* they do so. Anuruddha's reply describes their shared way of life, which seems to be the natural outward expression of their oneness of mind:

> *Venerable sir, as to that, whichever of us returns first from the village with almsfood prepares the seats, sets out the water for drinking and for washing, and puts the refuse bucket in its place. Whichever of us returns last eats any food left over, if he wishes; otherwise he throws it away where there is no greenery or drops it into water where there is no life. He puts away the seats and the water for drinking and for washing. He puts away the refuse bucket*

after washing it and he sweeps out the refectory. Whoever notices
that the pots of water for drinking, washing, or the latrine are low or
empty takes care of them. If they are too heavy for him, he calls
someone else by a signal of the hand and they move it by joining
hands, but because of this we do not break out into speech. But every
five days we sit together all night discussing the Dhamma. That is
how we abide diligent, ardent, and resolute.[25]

The three friends help one another by wordlessly doing whatever
needs to be done. In this way, they can maintain silence – an important aid to their meditation – while living a communal life. In
fact the silence not only supports their meditation, but also helps
them to develop a sensitive awareness of each other's needs.
When one sees that something needs doing, he just does it, without pausing to calculate whether the distribution of labour is fair,
or to check that the others are doing their share. All the same, the
silence is a means, not an end in itself, and therefore is not absolute: they regularly talk about the Dharma, for the opportunity to
do so is one of the main advantages of living together.

The Buddha expresses his approval of the three friends'
way of life, and enquires what spiritual fruits it has produced: he
asks them, 'But while you abide thus ... have you attained any
superhuman state, a distinction in knowledge and vision worthy
of the noble ones?' Replying on behalf of the others, Anuruddha
now reveals that all three of them have passed through the whole
range of spiritual and transcendental attainments. In other
words, they are all *arahants* – fully enlightened. The Buddha is
delighted by this wonderful news.

Eventually, after some further talk, he leaves them. At this
point, Nandiya and Kimbila have a question for Anuruddha.
While listening to the confident account of their attainments that
he gave to the Buddha, they were both thinking the same thing:
that, as far as they could recall, the three of them had never discussed that particular subject. To check their recollection, they

ask Anuruddha, 'Have we ever told you that we have achieved all those things that you credited us with?'

In reply, Anuruddha admits that the other two have never actually told him as much. Nevertheless he knows their 'abidings and attainments' by 'encompassing' their minds with his own. In other words, he has direct knowledge of their inner states, without any need for words. (To leave no doubt, he adds that deities have confirmed his perception.)

Anuruddha was to become renowned in the Buddhist tradition for his psychic powers. However, that fact does not explain why this conversation among the friends, after the Buddha's departure, was recorded in the *sutta*. It must be there in the discourse for a reason. Presumably its purpose is to underline the idea that the three 'are different in body, but one in mind'. The fact that Anuruddha can speak confidently of Nandiya's and Kimbila's spiritual attainments, without having heard them say anything on the subject, suggests that the expression 'one in mind' is not just a figure of speech but more literally true than we might have guessed.

The meaning of sangha

The story of the three friends shows us spiritual friendship as simultaneously belonging both to the path and the goal. Indeed, the discourse seems to suggest that there is a kind of ascending spiral, in which a life lived in friendship leads upwards to spiritual realization, which in turn bears the fruit of deeper friendship and fuller mutual communion.

In the example of Anuruddha, Nandiya, and Kimbila, we see kalyāṇa mitratā uniting a group of three disciples so that they form a circle of friendship. This reminds us that, while friendship is essentially a relationship between two people, it is by no means an exclusive relationship. A friend is free to have other friends, and two friends may have mutual friends. Among people who are committed to the same spiritual ideal, this interlocking pattern of friendship is the natural state of affairs.

It seems to me that such a network of spiritual friends, united by their common orientation to the Buddha and the Dharma, is intrinsic to the meaning of what Buddhists call *sangha*. The word *sangha* signifies the Buddhist spiritual community. It is often said or implied that only monks count as part of the sangha. Actually, it would be more correct to say that monks constitute one sector of the spiritual community. Tradition also recognizes a wider *mahā* sangha, or 'great community', including the Buddha's lay disciples. And then there is the enlightened sangha, which is spoken of variously (depending on which school of Buddhism is concerned) as the *ārya* sangha or bodhisattva sangha. The enlightened sangha is not a subdivision of the monastic sangha, but bridges the divide between the monks and the laity, for in the scriptures of all schools we find references to lay disciples who are *āryas* or bodhisattvas.

But these definitions, while informing us whom we may expect to find in the sangha, don't tell us what the sangha essentially is. To be part of a sangha must be more than a matter of donning a yellow robe, or publicly reciting the formula of the refuges and precepts – more even than experiencing a certain spiritual insight that others have also experienced. After all, the meaning of sangha is 'community', and a community is something more than a category or class of individuals. The members of a community are united with one another in some way.

It might be argued that the members of the sangha are united 'spiritually' simply by a common relationship to the Buddha and the Dharma. But such unity would amount to no more than an abstract concept if it were never actualized through living human relationships. And given the nature of the spiritual ideal, those relationships will presumably be ones of mutual concern and mettā – relationships that will naturally, when circumstances permit, mature into friendship. This is why, to my mind, friendship is intrinsic to the meaning of sangha. Admittedly, it is not usually practically possible (even within a single locality) for every member of the sangha to be a personal friend of every other. Nevertheless, it seems to me that an individual only truly participates in the sangha by means of friendship with at least some of its other members.

The friendships that make up a sangha naturally tend to grow. They grow in depth as friends get to know each other better, and as they tread more and more of the spiritual path in one another's company. Such friendships also tend to grow in number: new connections are formed within the existing sangha, and the sangha naturally attracts new members. In fact, if friendships are, as I am suggesting, the substance of sangha, it follows that the growth of a sangha can't really be measured simply by the increase in the number of individuals who avow their allegiance to a particular Buddhist teacher, or a particular presentation of the Dharma, or set of practices. The real growth of a sangha consists in the entry of individuals into this web of friendships.

Among other things, the purpose of the story of Anuruddha, Nandiya, and Kimbila is to show us something of the nature of sangha. The description of their life together offers a kind of snapshot of an ideal sangha in miniature. To participate in the sangha (at its highest) is to lead a life like that shared by these three: to dwell in such harmony with spiritual friends as to become 'one in mind' with them. This is indeed a high ideal – perhaps one that we don't find easy to imagine as a living reality. But while the loftiness of the ideal may be a little daunting, it does serve to show clearly the direction in which we need to go if we want to know for ourselves the deeper meaning of sangha.

The enlightened members of the spiritual community, such as Anuruddha and his two friends, are a kind of higher Sangha within the sangha. This higher Sangha (sometimes distinguished in writing by a capital S) is in fact one of the Three Jewels, the three most precious things in Buddhism, along with the Buddha and the Dharma. This brings us to a point worth pondering. The fact that Buddhism chooses to honour *three* things as centrally important suggests that the essential core of Buddhism cannot be satisfactorily encapsulated in a single image or idea, and that we will only understand it when we have looked at it from three viewpoints – viewing it 'in the round', so to speak. The Buddha jewel represents the spiritual ideal as embodied in a human individual. The Dharma jewel is the spiritual ideal viewed in the abstract as ultimate truth and spiritual means. The Sangha jewel is the spiritual ideal as embodied in those who are advanced on the spiritual path. But I think we will miss the full significance of the Sangha jewel if we think of it as merely a category or class of individuals. To my mind, the sangha (with or without the capital S) is a living organism, and its lifeblood is spiritual friendship.

In some cases, of course, circumstances may limit or even deny the personal contact that a committed Buddhist can have with others: there may not be any other Buddhists around! Nevertheless, anyone who genuinely goes for refuge to the Buddha and the Dharma carries at least the potential of spiritual friendship, like a seed, within his or her heart, destined to take root and grow whenever it finds the right soil and climate. In the story of Anuruddha, Nandiya, and Kimbila, we have one image of a Buddhist spiritual community in its ideal form; and it is without doubt an image of spiritual friendship.

3
Echoes and Silences

Friendship in the Buddhist Tradition

Friendship or solitude?

Many people imagine that the Buddhist ideal of human perfection, far from being one of friendship, is a cool, self-sufficient detachment. Those who think this way sometimes point to the centrepiece of Buddhist iconography as evidence, suggesting that a spirit of withdrawal is expressed by the solitary and self-contained nature of the Buddha image, with its impassive features and half-veiled eyes. They also call on the witness of certain Buddhist scriptures that speak with enthusiasm of the blessings of solitude.

As a matter of fact, Buddha images are not always solitary. In Buddhist art, the Buddha is often depicted accompanied by his two chief disciples, Sāriputta and Moggallāna, who appear as smaller figures flanking him, with their hands raised towards him, palms pressed together in the gesture of respectful salutation. Such statues and paintings are, in effect, representations of the Buddha and the Sangha, incorporating the vertical and horizontal axes of spiritual friendship in a single image.

As for the solitary Buddha image, perhaps we misunderstand it by viewing it as art in the modern Western sense. Nowadays, we automatically see all art as 'framed', and locate ourselves outside the frame, observing the scene through a sort of two-way mirror that lets us spy on the inhabitants of the image-world, without being seen by them. But traditionally, the Buddha image *stands for* the Buddha: the image brings you into his presence, and he sees you as clearly as you see him. In some traditions, monks meditating in a shrine-room sit in two rows facing each other, with the Buddha image between them at one end: everyone is turned towards the spiritual community, with the Buddha as its head. Similarly, the practices (common to all schools of Buddhism) of bowing and making offerings to the image express the same idea of the mutual presence of Buddha and sangha. Rather than exemplifying aloof detachment, the Buddha image brings Buddhists together with the Buddha.

It is true that solitude is often praised in the scriptures, and is highly valued in Buddhist practice. However, its value is as a means, not an end. Periods of withdrawal from human company – including perhaps some very lengthy periods – can help us to go deeper in meditation, and to discover who we really are when we are not trying to be what others want us to be. The experience of solitude is thus a necessary part of the journey towards psychological and spiritual independence.

Nevertheless, it seems that the value of such periods of solitude lies in their contribution to a larger or longer-term pattern of spiritual development, in which human communication and friendship also play a fundamental part. The scriptures we have looked at so far certainly support this view. The tale of Meghiya and the mango grove showed us that, for the average disciple, a close and deep association with spiritual friends is necessary before solitary meditation can progress very far. And even those who have already attained the 'liberation of the heart', such as Anuruddha, Nandiya, and Kimbila, consider it a 'great gain' to live with spiritual friends.

It seems that fellowship and solitude both contribute to the practice of Buddhism, and if we must assign a final priority to one or the other, we would do better to think of the spiritual life in terms of fellowship punctuated by solitude, rather than vice versa. The opposite view – that solitude is more fundamental – would not only run counter to the Buddha's teachings on spiritual friendship. It would also be hard to reconcile with the compassionate outlook that is intrinsic to the enlightened mind (as all schools agree, with varying degrees of emphasis). It would be very difficult to benefit living beings if one were firmly resolved to have as little as possible to do with them!

But what about those scriptures that sing the praises of solitary life? Perhaps the most famous Buddhist *sutta* (discourse) on this theme is the one whose refrain urges us to 'live alone, like a rhinoceros's horn'.[26] But the *Rhinoceros Horn Sutta* does not really recommend complete abstinence from human contact as the ideal way of life. To understand the discourse properly, we must remember that it was addressed to a particular audience: monks who had 'gone forth from the household life' (i.e. renounced conventional society), many of whom must have sometimes needed encouragement to sustain their ascetic vocation. The single horn of the Indian rhino, which gives the sutta its title and its refrain, is implicitly contrasted with the two horns of other horned beasts – a symbolic way of contrasting the unattached independence of the monk with the 'two-ness' of the married state. The independent habits of the rhino (which roams freely around its foraging territory, either alone or in small social groups) probably add something to the symbolism, evoking the ascetic lifestyle favoured by the Buddha and his early monastic disciples, who wandered from village to village in search of alms.

The *Rhinoceros Horn Sutta*, like many other early Buddhist discourses, is in verse. It began its life as an oral poem, designed not to be read in privacy, as we usually encounter it today (Buddhist scriptures remained unwritten for centuries after the Buddha's death), but to be recited aloud, to be heard from the lips of other monks, and to be learned by heart, perhaps at gatherings of the monastic sangha – facts that should remind us that the solitude praised in the sutta could hardly be absolute.

One of the purposes of the poem was to help and encourage the monks to stay true to their 'going forth', and to give up hankering for the intimacies of marriage and family life. Another purpose was to point out the distractions inherent in the ordinary variety of friendship. For example, some of the verses warn us that such bonds lead to time-consuming social obligations (being 'petitioned with requests'), frivolous pleasures (the 'love of amusement'), and unwholesome tendencies, such as trivial speech and quarrelling ('when I live with a second person, I am compelled to speak too much or to be angry with him').

But alongside this austere admonition to live free of worldly entanglements, the sutta presents a different and complementary message:

> *If one finds a wise friend, a companion living according to good virtues, prudent and having conquered all dangers, then live with him happily and mindfully....*
>
> *Certainly we praise the acquisition of friendship and friends – those who are either higher or equal in attainment or development should be associated with. Not finding such friends enjoying blameless food, let one live alone.*[7]

These words put the value of the solitary life in context. They suggest that, far from giving unqualified praise of solitude, the message of the *Rhinoceros Horn Sutta* is that indefinite solitude is a kind of default strategy: apparently it is only if we don't find 'higher or equal' spiritual friends (or in my terminology 'vertical or horizontal' ones) that we are meant to resort to living alone. And as we have seen, other scriptures offer us examples of disciples who live *together*, happily and to mutual advantage.

Friendship in practice: the Sigālaka Sutta

There are many other suttas in the Pali scriptures that refer to friendship. For example, in one group of discourses, the Buddha declares kalyāṇa mitratā to be the 'forerunner and precursor' of the arising of the noble eightfold path, and of the seven factors of enlightenment, just as the dawn signals the rising of the sun.[28]

Mostly, though, such suttas are brief statements in praise of spiritual friendship. They do not show us in any detail exactly what the Buddha meant by 'friendship'. Do any scriptures offer guidance on what in practice it means to be a friend?

The fullest discussion of this subject is to be found in the *Sigālaka Sutta* – the Buddha's teachings to Sigālaka on the social duties of ordinary life. Sigālaka is not a monk. In fact, at the start of the sutta he is not even a lay-follower of the Buddha (though he becomes one at the end): he seems to be an ordinary young man whom the Buddha happens to meet one morning. Consequently, in speaking to Sigālaka, the Buddha does not use the words 'kalyāṇa mitratā' (which assume a shared spiritual ideal). Nevertheless, the sutta casts much light on the Buddha's general idea of friendship.[29]

The central part of the discourse explains the obligations involved in each of six fundamental human relationships: those between friend and friend, husband and wife, parent and child, employer and employee, student and teacher, and disciple and spiritual guide. But the sutta treats friendship at greater length than the five other relationships, for the Buddha gives Sigālaka detailed preliminary advice on how to choose friends, identifying four types of bad friends to be avoided and four types of 'good-hearted friends' to be sought out and cultivated.[30]

The names by which the Buddha designates the four kinds of good-hearted friend immediately suggest a lot about his notion of friendship: 'the friend who is a helper', 'the friend who is the same in happy and unhappy times', 'the friend who points out what is good for you', and 'the friend who is sympathetic'. And in the subsequent description of these four types, we find a rich and rounded ideal of friendship, based on practical generosity, stead-fast loyalty, and empathy.

When we remember that the Buddha is here speaking to a non-Buddhist layman, we cannot help noticing that the ideal of friendship he presents to Sigālaka is surprisingly lofty, for the sutta shows clearly that the Buddha saw a significant moral and spiritual dimension even in ordinary friendship. We see this in the four qualities ascribed to 'the friend who points out what is good for you': he 'keeps you from wrongdoing, supports you in doing good, informs you of what you did not know, and ... points out the way to heaven'. In the context, the third of these qualities (that the friend 'informs you of what you did not know') is likely to mean that he shares his understanding of moral and spiritual matters.[31] Remarkably, this list of qualities is very similar to the duties later ascribed to 'ascetics and Brahmins', implying that, in the Buddha's view, a real friend is one who encourages your spiritual development in a way comparable to a religious guide.[32]

Sigālaka learns that friendship goes beyond mere mutual usefulness. For example, the Buddha seems to recognize the subtler, psychological benefits of intimacy: a good friend, he says, is someone who, among other things, 'tells you his secrets ... [and] guards your secrets'.[33] Loyalty is also valued: friendship includes 'being a refuge when [the friend] is afraid [and] not deserting him when he is in trouble'.[34] The sutta even points towards an ideal of self-transcendence through friendship: a man should 'minister towards his friends' to the extent of 'treating them like himself'.[35]

A good friend 'would even sacrifice his life for you'.[36] Nothing as selfless as this is suggested in connection with any of the other five kinds of relationship.

Clearly, then, the Buddha thought the choice of friends was an important moral influence on the individual's life, and that friendship was spiritually significant – even horizontal friendship between ordinary people for whom spiritual concerns were not central. Accordingly, we would expect him to have attached even more importance to such friendships between the spiritually committed. Indeed, some of the same qualities that are praised in the *Sigālaka Sutta* reappear in a shorter discourse addressed to monks:

> *Monks, let a monk cultivate a friend whose ways are seven. What seven? He gives what is hard to give, does what is hard to do, bears what is hard to bear, confesses his own secret, keeps others', in want forsakes one not, despises not when one is ruined. Verily, monks, let a monk cultivate a friend whose ways are such.*[37]

Apart from references to friends and friendship, the scriptures have a lot to say on the importance of harmony in the sangha – suggesting that friendship is at the heart of the Buddhist conception of spiritual community. Many parts of the *Vinaya* (the compendium of monastic discipline) are concerned with how to maintain harmony and avoid or resolve disputes.

The Buddha also urged monks to cultivate and express love and friendliness (*mettā*) towards one another. For example, in teachings he gave near the end of his life, he taught various conditions that, if maintained, would allow the monastic sangha 'to prosper and not decline'. Among these was a set of 'six things that are conducive to communal living'.[38] The first three of the six urge the monks to maintain towards one another, whether in public or in private, acts of loving-kindness. (The first specifies bodily actions of this kind, while the second and third apply the same principle at the levels of speech and mind, respectively.) As we saw, Anuruddha and his friends followed this practice of maintaining loving deeds, words, and thoughts towards each other.

Praise of friendship in the Gaṇḍavyūha Sūtra

The texts I have mentioned so far are all from one body of scriptures – the Pali canon. In theory, all schools of Buddhism accept these scriptures (in versions distinguished from each other only by relatively minor differences). In practice, however, they receive little attention from the Mahāyāna schools of Tibet and eastern Asia, which have their own *sūtras*. However, spiritual friendship is fulsomely celebrated in one of the greatest of these – the *Gaṇḍavyūha* ('World Array') *Sūtra*. This spiritual epic was of great importance for Chinese Buddhism: incorporated as the climax of the vast 'Flower Ornament Scripture', it became the key text of the Hua Yen school. Many regard it as the supreme Buddhist teaching. Some of this enthusiasm has rubbed off on many Western Buddhists, who are fascinated by the *Gaṇḍavyūha's* doctrine of the mutual interpenetration of all things. However, another major (but less noted) theme of the sūtra is spiritual friendship.

The story concerns a young man called Sudhana, who aspires to become a bodhisattva – that is, someone dedicated to the attainment of enlightenment for the benefit of all beings. The sūtra shows how he comes to form this aspiration, and then describes his quest for spiritual friends who can help him to fulfil it. Inspired by his first friend, Mañjuśrī, he goes on to meet many more in the course of his travels, culminating with the great bodhisattva Maitreya ('Friendly One'). From each friend, Sudhana learns part of what he needs in order to become supremely enlightened.

Spiritual friendship is praised again and again by the bodhisattvas Sudhana meets on his journey. The most substantial of the many speeches about it comes from a pair called Srisambhava and Srimati. They begin by urging Sudhana to seek out the company of spiritual friends as much as possible, and to communicate with such friends as deeply and tirelessly as he can:

> O son of a noble family, you must be unwearied in your search for friends in the good life, you must never feel contented with (merely) seeing friends in the good life; you must never feel satisfied with (merely) conversing with friends in the good life; you must never abandon your intention of being in the company of friends in the good life.[39]

The conception of spiritual friendship here, as elsewhere in the sūtra, is predominantly vertical. Nevertheless, friends are always spoken of in the plural, and often in ways that seem to suggest the mutual support and encouragement of a spiritual community rather than a single teacher–student relationship:

> O son of a noble family, kept back by friends in the good life the Bodhisattvas do not fall into the pits of woeful existences; surrounded by friends in the good life the Bodhisattvas do not turn away from the Great Career (Mahāyāna); exhorted by friends in the good life the Bodhisattvas do not forsake the teachings of the Bodhisattvas, guarded by friends in the good life the Bodhisattvas do not come under the power of bad friends.[40]

The eulogy continues in poetic similes that echo, in many different keys, the Buddha's saying that kalyāṇa mitratā is the whole of the spiritual life:

> Furthermore, O son of a noble family, friends in the good life are a mother, because they give birth (to Bodhisattvas) in the Buddha families; friends in the good life are a father, because they bring immense good;... friends in the good life are a physician, because they free (the Bodhisattvas) from the disease of self-centred passion; friends in the good life are the Himalaya mountains because they

make the herb of knowledge grow; friends in the good life are heroes,
because they protect (the Bodhisattvas) against all dangers.[41]

The *Gaṇḍavyūha* is an allegory: the characters in its drama represent qualities and attainments. Mañjuśrī, for example, *is* wisdom. At the same time, Mañjuśrī is much more than a 'type': he is a *bodhisattva mahāsattva* – a 'great being dedicated to universal enlightenment'. Like others in the story, he not only symbolizes abstractions but also exemplifies the bodhisattva's behaviour as a spiritual friend. True, the allegorical style of the sūtra rarely makes us feel we are being shown a portrait 'from life' of actual friendship (as we do, for example, when we read the story of Anuruddha and his friends). Nevertheless, there are moments when the loving and mutually delighting quality of spiritual friendship is beautifully evoked.

One such moment occurs at Sudhana's first appearance in the story, amid an assembly listening to Mañjuśrī expound the Dharma. Mañjuśrī singles out Sudhana from the crowd to rejoice in his merits by commenting on his name. We learn that Sudhana ('Good Wealth') was so called because, at the time of his birth, astonishing treasuries of precious metals and stones – obviously symbols of merit accumulated in past lives – miraculously appeared in his parents' house. Mañjuśrī goes on to deliver to the assembly (and to Sudhana in particular) a discourse on 'all the elements of buddhahood'.[42] Here we see Mañjuśrī performing one of the functions of the ideal spiritual friend: he is making Sudhana aware, in a direct and personal way, of his own potential for Buddhahood. Listening to Mañjuśrī, Sudhana hears the call of the bodhisattva path.

Having concluded his discourse, Mañjuśrī makes to depart, but Sudhana cannot let him go. Lifted into an ecstasy of devotion, he spontaneously salutes Mañjuśrī with a poem, rejoicing in his virtues and powers, and pleading with him to 'set him upon the vehicle of enlightenment'. In response, Mañjuśrī advises Sudhana,

> *Attending and serving spiritual friends is the beginning, the logical course, for the accomplishment of omniscience. Therefore you should tirelessly attend spiritual benefactors.*[43]

And so he sends Sudhana off on the quest. Sudhana will return to Mañjuśrī at the end of the story, after his encounter with Maitreya. Meanwhile, he and Mañjuśrī go their separate ways; but the description of Sudhana's parting from Mañjuśrī depicts feelings of remarkable warmth and tenderness:

> *Then Sudhana, pleased, enraptured, transported with joy, delighted, happy, and cheerful, laid his head at the feet of Manjushri in respect, circled Manjushri hundreds and thousands of times, and looked at him hundreds and thousands of times, with a mind full of love for the spiritual friend, unable to bear not seeing the spiritual friend, with tears streaming down his face as he wept, and left Manjushri.*[44]

In the context of a Buddhist scripture, this display of affectionate tears may strike us as surprising. It might seem suggestive of attachment – often named as one of the greatest obstacles to the quest for enlightenment. However, we notice that Sudhana, although 'unable to bear not seeing the spiritual friend', is simultaneously 'cheerful', 'happy', even 'transported with joy'. Far from falling into gloom after Mañjuśrī's departure – as we might expect in a more ordinary 'attachment' – he sets out enthusiastically on a spiritual quest. If this can be called attachment at all, it is not of the ordinary kind, but a passionate attachment to the good, which the sūtra clearly intends us to regard as something wholesome and admirable.

Friendship in Buddhist Discourse

It is time to take stock of what we have found in the Buddhist scriptures on the subject of friendship. To begin with, the Buddha asserted on several occasions that kalyāṇa mitratā was the whole of the spiritual life. He also described, in outline, what we could call a 'fivefold path' of friendship to Meghiya and to others. He taught lay people and monks about the qualities and behaviour of a good friend. The scriptures also contain vivid and moving examples of friendship among the Buddha's disciples. Later, the Mahāyāna restated the importance of spiritual friendship with resounding, rhapsodic emphasis in the *Gaṇḍavyūha Sūtra*.

In view of such evidence, the idea that friendship is an important part of Buddhism seems to me quite orthodox. However, I can think of several possible reasons why the idea might seem unfamiliar and questionable to some.

I think many Buddhists understand the words 'kalyāṇa mitratā' too narrowly. This tendency has two aspects. The first is the reduction of kalyāṇa mitratā to the vertical kind, forgetting the horizontal. The second is the interpretation of the vertical kind as a relatively impersonal relationship between teacher and student, characterized perhaps by instruction or the ritual transmission of power. Important as such relationships may be for many Buddhists, I don't think they exhaust the possibilities of vertical kalyāṇa mitratā. Perhaps the equation of kalyāṇa mitra with 'teacher' would not have been a problem in India in the Buddha's day, when (if the *Sigālaka Sutta* is anything to go by) teachers' relationships with their students were less distant, more cordial, and much more sustained – and to that extent more like friendship – than they are in our culture. In Western society, a teacher belongs (like a doctor or a lawyer) to the class of professionals – technical specialists who are not supposed to get too personally involved with their clients, and with whom one's relationship usually ends once their professional function has been discharged. When we read the word 'teacher' in a Buddhist text, we may fail to catch the undertone of friendship.

For Buddhists in the English-speaking world, the under-valuing of spiritual friendship may have been compounded by questionable translations. As I mentioned in Chapter 1, there are certain English translations of the Pali scriptures in which we find 'kalyāṇa mitratā' rendered as, for example, 'friendship with what is lovely'. This obscures the fact that the Buddha was speaking of personal relationships. (This question of translation is discussed in the Appendix.)

There are other reasons, too. Although the scriptural references are clear and emphatic, it is easy to overlook them in the vast body of Buddhist canonical literature. The theme of friendship echoes through the suttas, but the echoes are intermitted by long silences. Perhaps the most important reason friendship does not leap out of the scriptures as a prominent theme is that these scattered references were never integrated and elaborated in one systematic account (in the way that the *Satipaṭṭhāna Sutta*, for example, seems to gather and systematize a range of teachings on mindfulness).

But some might still pose the question of why no great Buddhist teacher, in the millennia since the Buddha's passing away, has picked up the theme. Despite the high profile given to friendship in some canonical texts, Buddhism has had little to say on the subject in its later literature. The great minds of the Buddhist tradition seem, in the main, either to have passed it over in silence, or to have treated it in a way that reinforced the tendency to interpret 'spiritual friend' narrowly as 'teacher'.

It seems that, historically, Buddhists simply have not felt much need to discuss friendship. But the absence of discussion does not mean that there was no friendship. Friendship may not have kept up a prominent place in Buddhist discourse, but it must always have been part of Buddhist life. The most likely explanation of the silence is that the meaning and value of friendship were too obvious, and its expression too natural, to require any theorizing. In the scriptures, for example, the subject of mindfulness receives extensive and systematic treatment, because mindfulness has never been easy. Friendship, while explicitly recognized as vitally important, was treated only briefly because most people needed little or no coaching in it.

But if friendship was straightforward for Buddhists in times gone by, that does not mean it remains so today. Changes in the social context of Buddhist life may require changes of emphasis in Buddhist teaching. Such new emphases need not entail any distortion of fundamental principles: it is in the nature of the Dharma to express its universal meaning differently in different times and places, according to the needs of the audience. This is the essence of 'skilful means' (*upāya kauśalya*) – an important concept in the Mahāyāna. If modern Buddhism develops the theme of spiritual friendship, it will be following in the time-honoured Buddhist tradition of elaborating something that the Buddha taught only 'in brief'.

I think Buddhists today do need to pay more attention to spiritual friendship, and to discuss and explore what it means. This need for emphasis and exploration is indeed new, though the importance of friendship itself is timeless. Inevitably, the question arises of why things have changed. If friendship could be taken for granted in the past, why can't it any longer? Why is it only now, and among Western Buddhists, that some of us have begun to feel we must stress friendship explicitly, and talk about its significance?

I think the answer is that in the modern world friendship has declined in importance in our way of life. This decline is most advanced in the West, but it is spreading as the rest of the world becomes Westernized. Few realize that anything has been lost, because the decay of friendship has been drawn out over several generations, and has taken place in an era of prosperity that has brought abundant material gains to console us for our loss. But the loss is real.

In order to establish itself in a new culture, Buddhism must first find (or create for itself) the conditions it needs to grow. At the moment, the seed of the Dharma is spreading rapidly in the West, but whether it is putting down deep roots remains to be seen. In some ways, it is struggling in a soil that differs from any it has been planted in before. One of the missing nutrients is friendship.

4
The Torn Net

Friendship in Crisis

The Western tradition of friendship

At this point, we have to make an abrupt scene-shift – from Buddhist scriptures to Western social history. William is writing to his friend Edward:

> Here is the third letter I have begun, dear Edward, in reply to that noble one which I have just received from you – the two first were full of thanks, but I had better leave you to [imagine] these, finding it myself so difficult to describe them. What I like to think of better than your generosity or the cause of it, is the noble and brotherly love which I believe unites us together; my dear friend,... may God grant that no time or circumstance ever should diminish this love between us; it seems to me a thing which one should cultivate and preserve as a virtue, as a kind of religion, of which it seems to have usurped the place.[45]

Perhaps you can't guess exactly when this letter dates from, but there is one thing you will be sure of: it was not written by anyone

born into our era. To modern taste, the writer's warmth and idealism in expressing friendship is likely to sound rather effusive. *We*
don't talk or write to our friends in such a way. And that isn't just
a matter of reticence: we probably don't have the same kind of
feeling.

The letter was written in October 1834 by the novelist
William Thackeray to his friend Edward Fitzgerald. Reading the
letter today, we might wonder whether the author's feelings
were 'really' – that is, unconsciously – sexual. Thackeray's modern biographers don't seem to think so, but of course no certain
answer to this question is possible. All we can say is that the two
men's friendship seems to have been an exhilarated meeting of
minds rather than a love affair. When they were together, they
spent their time enthusiastically discussing religion, art, literature, and music.[46]

Many more quotations expressing the same spirit of friendship could be culled from the literature and correspondence of
times past. Most of them would record the writings or utterances
of men, because until fairly recent times it was mainly men who
acquired the education and confidence needed to reflect on and
document their experience. But friendship was without doubt
important for women too. In the 1880s, Edith Simcox was able to
read some of the published correspondence of her late friend,
Marian Evans (better known under her pen-name, George Eliot).
Her response reveals both tenderness and a touching pride in her
devotion:

> I am glad to know as much as possible of all Her friends. I am not
> sorry that I do not find amongst them all any to whom She Herself
> was more than She was and is to me.[47]

These writers' contemporaries would have seen nothing quaint
or questionable about the existence of such warm feelings
between friends of the same sex (even if the Victorian age became
increasingly reticent about men's expression of any strong

emotions). In fact, such feelings would have been thought healthy and admirable in most eras other than our own.

In the letter quoted above, Thackeray associates friendship with virtue. This too was commonplace. Admittedly, traditional piety might have frowned on his statement that friendship had 'usurped the place' of religion. Apart from that, though, his idea that friendship was noble and associated with goodness would have been perfectly intelligible to his own and earlier times. Until the twentieth century, educated people still looked on friendship in the light of an ancient tradition that regarded it as the finest of human bonds. Cultured people often gave it pride of place in their personal hierarchy of relationships. The learned doctor Thomas Browne, in one of the most admired and imitated essays of the seventeenth century, put it this way:

> I confess I do not observe that order that the schools ordain our affections, to love our parents, wives, children, and [only] then our friends, for excepting the injunctions of religion, I do not find in myself such a necessary and indissoluble sympathy to all those of my blood. I hope I do not break the fifth commandment, if I conceive I may love my friend before the nearest of my blood.[48]

The tradition went back a very long way – right back, in fact, to the roots of Western culture in the Bible and pagan antiquity, each of which provided ideal models of friendship. In the Old Testament, David and Jonathan each loved the other 'as his own soul'. Greek myth and drama provided a parallel archetype in the friendship of Orestes and Pylades, each willing to die for the other.

As well as setting such legendary examples, the ancient world also gave birth to the philosophical discussion of friendship. The classics in this tradition – ranging from Books Eight and Nine of Aristotle's Ethics to Cicero's On Friendship – remained well known throughout the Middle Ages. This theoretical examination of friendship seems to have arisen not because friendship had become problematic in any way, but as part of the Greek philosophical project to develop a complete account of nature, man, and society by purely rational means.

From the late sixteenth to the early nineteenth century, the prestige of friendship in European culture increased, if anything. At the beginning of this period, Montaigne and Bacon wrote famous essays in praise of it. As for the seventeenth and eighteenth centuries, they 'elaborated friendship and all but made it their religion', according to the modern writer Cyril Connolly.[49] Like any religion, of course, this one sometimes degenerated into conventional piety, mere lip service to an ideal. Nevertheless, for many people – Thackeray is a good example – friendship was clearly not just a literary pose, but a deeply felt experience. It would be easy to produce many more instances of the warmth and high seriousness that people used to bring to their friendships before our times, so many that it is implausible to dismiss them all as genuflections to a lifeless idol.

But we don't seem to speak of friendship – or, for the most part, feel it – so passionately now. It is hard to avoid the impression that the institution of friendship must have suffered a decline in the West throughout the later nineteenth and the twentieth centuries. Today, in the morning of the twenty-first, how many of us would claim that it features prominently in our life, either as ideal or experience?

Nets and atoms: tradition and modernity

My examples so far have been drawn from the educated strata of Western society, but the vitality of friendship in pre-modern culture was not confined to such circles. Friendship is, as the social scientists put it, 'cross-cultural', a distinct 'institution' recognized in a wide range of societies as a 'voluntary, close, and enduring social relationship', involving 'commitment, intimacy, and spontaneity', whose 'consequences for the individual and for society, through individual growth and security, are presumably crucial'.[50]

Modern Westerners who work in developing countries often become exasperated with the unfairness and corruption of cultures based on what the Chinese call *guanxi* – 'personal connections'. Nevertheless, the observant ones sometimes notice that the inhabitants of those countries are less troubled by the loneliness, anxiety, and meaninglessness that often haunt us in the developed world. Strangely, those who are poor (and perhaps unjustly governed) are often more cheerful, warm-hearted, and generous than citizens of the advanced economies. This is not just a product of their modest expectations; it has a more positive source in their sense of being a valued part of a web of human connections.

My friend Sudarshan, an Indian member of the order to which I belong, now in his late fifties, has some interesting things to say about friendship in India. As a leading order member, he has plenty of friends in the Buddhist community. His role in the sangha keeps him very busily concerned with their spiritual needs. Nevertheless, he somehow manages to keep in touch with friends from all the early phases of his life – village, school, and college – nurturing old friendships in a way that many Westerners wouldn't bother with. Whenever he returns to his home village, he visits his childhood friends; and if he happens to be in a town where an old college friend lives, he usually looks him up.

Looking back, Sudarshan can see that friendship was also very important to his parents and their generation. His family belongs to a caste that was once labelled with the cruel tag 'untouchable'. But despite the fearsome power of the caste system in India, some of his parents' closest friendships crossed the caste barrier. He particularly remembers his father's friend Devaji: it seemed that between the two of them there were few, if any, secrets. Such intimacy, he thinks, was more common between friends than between members of a family, for tensions and rivalry within the family (especially those stemming from the age-hierarchy between siblings) made the formation of intimate bonds easier with friends than with blood relatives.

Sudarshan particularly remembers a tough period in his childhood during which his mother was afflicted by tuberculosis. It went on for three years. During that time the family needed a lot of help from friends. And they got it. At times, friends even did the hard work of ploughing their fields for them.

Having in recent years got to know a lot of Westerners, and visited the West several times, Sudarshan's impression is that on the whole (and setting aside the Buddhist world that he and I share) friendship is much more important in India than in the West. This doesn't mean that Indians are necessarily better at every aspect of friendship: when Indian friends quarrel, the danger of a bitter and lasting rift is greater. It is harder to reconcile them, especially if they feel they have lost face in the row. In general, though, friendship does seem to come more naturally to them than to Westerners.

Nevertheless, Sudarshan sees that things are changing rapidly: the younger generation in India are getting more like Westerners – more educated, more confident, and with higher material expectations. They seem to pay less attention to friends.

In traditional cultures, human beings experience themselves less as isolated individuals than as parts of a network of relationships that extends in all directions. The knots holding the strands of the net together are enduring, indeed lifelong. In some cultures, the collective imagination, embodied in myth and folklore, may extend the web into the past to include ancestors, legendary founders, and deities. In this way, individuals dwell in a sense of solidarity with the universe as a whole. In such a world, the institution of friendship naturally holds an honoured place.

This must have been the normal human condition, in both East and West, until as recently as the early nineteenth century.

Then things started to change with the industrial revolution, the growth of the market economy, and the social upheaval that came in their wake. The new economy substituted a simple, impersonal 'cash nexus' for old, complex social obligations. Vast numbers of people pulled up their roots in small communities and set off to pursue material security or betterment. Many of them poured into the anonymous existence of teeming cities. The threads of family and community began to unravel.

In the second half of the twentieth century, this trend accelerated. The extraordinary prosperity of the developed countries in that period encouraged people to throw off old restraints to pursue private desires and ambitions. At the same time, new forms of material security – insurance policies, pensions, and welfare systems – removed much of the pressure of necessity that used to maintain the bonds of family and friendship.

Many countries and their citizens now measure their success in terms of the consumption of resources. This value system encourages us to be high-spending consumers who live in small units, or even alone. Official statistics in the UK, for example, show that in the three decades preceding 2001 the number of one-person households (not counting the elderly) tripled to 15% of all households.[51] At the same time, modern economies require a fluid labour market, in which the efficient matching of jobs with appropriate hands or brains must not be restrained by strong loyalties to places or persons. Consequently, we have become, by the standards of former times, remarkably mobile in our pursuit of happiness. The same statistical source reveals that the average person in Britain stays in one place for only five to ten years before moving elsewhere. (And within the five-year period of the survey, one in ten adults moved house every year.)[52]

The last few paragraphs are, no doubt, a rather sweeping summary of the social trends of the last two centuries, and many 'buts' could be inserted in it. Nevertheless, I believe it to be fair in essentials. Probably the most significant of all the social changes of the last century is what might be called social atomization: the modern human being increasingly resembles an isolated atom of selfhood, a free centre of desire and action, independently seeking fulfilment. This can be exhilarating and, in a sense, 'empowering', but at the same time it inevitably spells a decline in the permanence and importance of human relationships. In the developed world, over the last two centuries, the human net has been badly torn. The same process is now well advanced in many developing countries too. As the historian Eric Hobsbawm has put it:

> The world was now tacitly assumed to consist of several billion human beings defined by their pursuit of individual desire.... The cultural revolution of the later twentieth century can thus best be understood as the triumph of the individual over society, or rather, the breaking of the threads which in the past had woven human beings into social textures.[53]

Hobsbawm calls the culture that this revolution has produced 'anomic society' (presumably echoing the sociologist Durkheim's famous concept of anomie – the absence of generally shared social norms or moral values). The ills of anomic society – divorce, single parent families, drug abuse, high suicide rates, and so on – are too well known to require rehearsal here. Such things are just the more visible symptoms of a deeper malaise. They only affect a minority, if a worryingly large one. But the underlying condition affects us all: human relationships are weaker than in the past – more distant, more transitory, and more fragile.

Can we therefore conclude that friendship declined as a social institution during the twentieth century? In a strictly scientific sense, we can't know for certain whether this is true or not. The hard data that might prove the case either way don't exist. The social sciences – to which we might go for a statistical answer – only began to pay attention to friendship (in a limited way) when the twentieth century was quite well advanced. In any case, friendship is a subtle, elusive thing, not easily pinned down quantitatively. Nevertheless, from what we know of the general nature of social and cultural change in the period, it does seem that the conditions for friendship are now much less propitious than in earlier times.

The Buddhist perspective

All people of goodwill must feel at least some concern about the process of social atomization. But what exactly are we to think of it, and how should we respond? We can't go back to the traditional world, and wouldn't want to. Should we just accept anomic society as part of the price of prosperity and personal freedom?

These questions have a special irony for the small but growing number of Westerners who have become Buddhists, or who find in Buddhism a source of moral and spiritual inspiration. The existence of this group has become possible partly because of the very breakdown of tradition that has produced anomic society. Religion, like so many things, is now a matter of individual choice.

Having grown up in it, Western Buddhists – like other Westerners – tend to take anomic society for granted. While acknowledging a few problems, they endorse it as progress. On the whole, they are right. But it is worth pausing sometimes to remember that what the Buddha took for granted was traditional society, founded on a network of personal relationships, not the atomized one we are familiar with. We can only speculate what the Buddha would have thought of our age. I imagine he would have acknowledged our improvements in nutrition, medicine, education, and many other areas. At the same time, I can't see him being wholly enthusiastic about modern society, in which the pursuit of material self-interest has moved nearer to the top of our table of values.

It is instructive to compare our world with the one posited by the *Sigālaka Sutta*, which I discussed in Chapter 3. Friendship is one of a pattern of six fundamental relationships discussed in the sutta, namely those with parents, teachers, spouse and children, friends, servants or employees, and religious teachers. The Buddha encouraged Sigālaka to think of these relationships as guarding the six directions of space (that is, the four cardinal points, together with the zenith and nadir). Parents, for example, can be seen as guarding the east (the direction of the sunrise and thus of origins), spouse and children in the west, religious teachers in the zenith, and so on. Sigālaka was also urged by the Buddha to pay homage to – one could even say 'worship' – the six relationships, as symbolized by the six directions.

Implicit in this is the idea that a healthy human life is located within and supported by an ordered universe of relationships, each marked by its characteristic set of responsibilities and rewards. The social world depicted in the sutta certainly has a remarkable universality: the six relationships are still recognizable today. According to the Buddha, each of the six requires respect and care if one's existence is to be secure and happy.

In the *Sigālaka Sutta* the Buddha was addressing lay people, living in families, for whom spiritual concerns were not central. What about those men and women who chose to dedicate themselves to the spiritual life? Did they become free-floating social atoms? Far from it. When a young man (for example) left his parents to join the monastic spiritual community, he would inevitably take with him a sense of organic connection to a social world. Within the monastic sangha, of course, the pattern of relationships around him would be different: there would be no wife or child; the bond with his parents would at least be attenuated. But existence within a network of relationships would continue: the new monk's prior experience of close bonds with family and friends would be the foundation for kalyāṇa mitratā within the spiritual community. Feelings of brotherhood for equals, protective care for juniors, and grateful respect for elders could relatively easily be transferred to those who occupied analogous roles in the sangha. And wherever the monastic community was spiritually vital, such feelings would not just be transferred to, but might also be transmuted by, the new situation. The iron of ordinary friendship might become the gold of spiritual friendship.

We can now understand why the Buddha saw no need to spell out the theory and practice of friendship. He did find it necessary to highlight friendship from time to time, especially when dealing with individualists like Meghiya. Most disciples, however, needed little encouragement to form friendships, and no guidance on how to go about it. Ordinary life equipped them with the necessary outlook and habits, which the spiritual life simply took over.

By the same token, we can begin to see how an explicit emphasis on friendship might be helpful for the practice of the Dharma in our times. Meghiya, by the standards of his day, was an individualist. That is why he needed a lesson in friendship. Nowadays, however, individualism is the norm. As children of anomic society, we are more inclined to think of number one: consciously or unconsciously, we look for ways to maximize our freedom and minimize our obligations. We undervalue friendship, and consequently many of us don't have a very deep or sustained experience of it.

Friendship in crisis

Of the six fundamental relationships identified in the *Sigālaka Sutta*, the one worst hit by anomic society is probably the relationship with religious guides, but next to these friendship is the most serious casualty. I don't want to exaggerate the crisis. Friendship is by no means dead: it is a part of human nature and could never die. Even in our era, it is still quite robust here and there – perhaps especially among younger people before they settle into marriage, family, and career responsibilities. But the signs suggest to me that on the whole friendship is not thriving. People have friends, but don't necessarily keep them throughout life, or see them very frequently, or place them in the first rank of importance among their relationships.

It therefore seems that friendship has fared worse from the ravages of social atomization than have relationships between marriage partners, or between parents and children (although these have suffered too). Why has friendship come off so badly? There are many reasons, but I am going to discuss a few that seem important to me.

Firstly, we are prone to imagine that friendship is superfluous. One aspect of the atomization of society is that, far from being its helpless victims, most of us embrace the values of individualism to some degree. We fear being trapped or tied down. Modern life is a competitive game for any number of players. People naturally want to maximize their income, their status, and their enjoyment of the pleasures of life. There are subtler stakes in the game, but these too are often conceived and pursued as commodities: job satisfaction and so on. We know that to get the most from the game, we need to retain our freedom and autonomy, which means not investing too much in personal ties, while trying to avoid becoming too lonely.

The culture of individualism hurts friendship more than the other relationships because friendship is more voluntary and less anchored in biological necessity than the others. The nuclear family is portable (or at least, people hope it will be). But friendship is the most disposable, despite being the most distinctively human, of bonds. The Christian writer C.S. Lewis, lamenting the modern decline of friendship, neatly summed the point up when he wrote, 'Without Eros none of us would have been begotten and without Affection none of us would have been reared; but we can live and breed without friendship.'[54]

Secondly, there are the effects of the last century's sexual revolution. To point out that this has also brought some problems in its wake is by no means to make a plea for a return to 'Victorian values'. Today, we probably enjoy more sexual freedom than any previous age. In general, this does not create a very favourable climate for friendship, for sex competes to some extent with friendship as an expression of human relatedness. For example, a busy sex life can provide an easy substitute for deeper forms of personal intimacy that may seem too challenging. And for many people, emotional intimacy has become so closely linked to sexual desire that it is only looked for in that context.

However, the sexual revolution also poses a subtler obstacle to friendship than these, namely our sophisticated awareness of the way in which sexual interest may be present in non-sexual relationships. Nowadays, we are prone to suspect a sexual motivation in any same-sex friendship that is significantly warmer and closer than average. This tendency probably started with Freud, who saw the sexual drive as the primary motivating force behind all human behaviour. The popularization of Freud's ideas has merged seamlessly with modern sexual liberalism and the commercialization of sex. Today, sex looms larger in our self-understanding, and in our interpretation of the behaviour of others, than it did in bygone ages. No doubt this has freed us from much naivety and quite a few hang-ups, but at the same time it has added something to the cultural trend that makes us cooler in same-sex friendships than our forebears.

By 1960, this tendency had become so marked that C.S. Lewis, in his book *The Four Loves*, found it necessary to preface his chapter on friendship with a few pages of careful logical demolition of the idea that strong friendships must 'really' be homosexual.[55] By 1983, Stuart Miller, an American writer who was preparing a book about men and friendship, was being warned off the project by an academic mentor, who told him that people would assume that the book was about homosexuality, which 'could be dangerous' to his future.[56]

The idea that homosexual desire might be at the root of strong friendly feelings causes anxiety to some of us, perhaps especially to young people who are uncertain of their own identity, and anxious to conform to peer pressure. Despite growing tolerance in law and in educated opinion, popular culture continues to stigmatize homosexual desire, and male homosexuals in particular are often seen as failing to live up to crude but widely current notions of masculinity. Anxiety about becoming the object of such perceptions is hardly likely to enhance the growth of warmth and intimacy between people of the same sex. While these inhibitions are not usually strong enough to destroy friendship, they may restrict it to a superficial camaraderie, in which deeper feelings are left unexpressed.

Of course, the sexual drive is a much more pervasive and fundamental force than Victorian culture was willing to admit, but this doesn't mean that the roots of friendship are sexual. It may well be true that an erotic element is often unconsciously present in people's feelings towards friends of the same sex, but I suspect that nowadays the opposite also happens, that is, people often mistakenly interpret the feelings of warmth that arise in friendship as sexual, and may stifle them in consequence.

The third factor in the decline of friendship is to do with the cultural context in which sexuality is expressed. In the modern West, romantic love is widely regarded as the most important human bond. It is the relationship in which, more than any other, people now invest their hopes for a fulfilling existence – the flower blooming in the desert of a Godless world.

In former times, the art of friendship began in childhood and youth, and was brought to maturity in early adulthood. Most people still experience important friendships in childhood and youth, but as we grow up we absorb from the culture around us the assumption that romantic sexual love is the proper sphere for warmth, intimacy, and strong feelings. Under the influence of this belief, the friendships of our early years may come to seem, in hindsight, something to be grown out of, mere appetizers for the adult banquet of love. The conviction that friendship is tepid is likely to give us low expectations of it – which will naturally tend to fulfil themselves. With many people now becoming sexually active even in their early teens, friendship probably gets rather less chance to flower than it used to.

Our increasing reliance on romantic love stems partly from the disappearance of the traditional division between men's world and women's world. In so far as this has brought freedom to women, it is undeniably a good thing. The trouble is that we have not yet recognized and addressed its consequences for friendship. In the days when men and women had distinct roles and interests in life, the need for friends of one's own sex seemed obvious: there were all sorts of things that could be shared only with them. Nowadays, women are likely to be as well educated as men (better, in fact) and are often just as ambitious in their careers; conversely, men are expected to take a bigger share in child-rearing duties. The worlds of the sexes now substantially overlap. How natural it seems to us – and how convenient in our busy lives – that one's spouse or lover should also be one's best friend. Are other close friends really necessary?

Many adults settled in marriages or long-term sexual partnerships engage in most of their social activities as a two-some. Perhaps at some level they feel that it would be rude or dis-loyal to their partner to invest too much time or emotion in a private intimacy – even of a non-sexual kind – outside the mar-riage. The couple seems now to be the standard unit of social life. Two old friends may see little of each other without the presence of two extra people, so their friendship may slowly fade in depth and importance, starved of opportunities to renew the kind of intimacy that flows more easily *tête-à-tête*.

The fourth factor contributing to the decline of friendship is the fading of shared ideals. Ideals are closely related to *values*, so their decline is implicit in the very idea of 'anomic society'. To say that people today are less idealistic does not necessarily mean that they are more selfish (although that may indeed be one effect of social atomization). Clearly there are still many people who feel an urge to make life better for others, and who try to do something about it.

But current ideas of a better life tend to be limited. They are often confined to goals that are materially redistributive in nature: that is, they aim at a fairer sharing of goods, services, or legal rights. Some people want to eliminate sex discrimination, some fight for animal rights, and so on. I share the desire for a more just society, but I doubt whether this kind of idealism alone can satisfy what is deepest in the human heart.

There is another kind of idealism – a kind that seems to me less in favour today – in which the ideal appeals to the individual 'from above', speaking of something more than material well-being or an equitable distribution of goods. Certain forms of patriotic or religious idealism belong in this category. (One example, of course, is Buddhism, which doesn't primarily aim to organize self-interest rationally and fairly, but rather to relinquish it altogether.) Admittedly, this higher kind of idealism often takes dangerous forms. A world devoid of it would be free of crusades, inquisitions, and many other bad things; but free too of great reformers and educators, free of certain kinds of artist, free of saints and bodhisattvas.

In a cultural climate that lacks this higher sort of idealism, some varieties of friendship can still grow well enough, but other varieties don't really thrive. Friendship needs to be about something. That is, it generally springs from a common interest. Without shared idealism, the only ground on which friendship can build is mutual practical usefulness or shared pleasure. But those kinds of interest don't necessarily last, and may not engage the heart or mind very deeply. Consequently the friendships that grow out of them don't always live very long, or rise very high. But we are straying into an area that I am going to explore fully in the next chapter.

The fifth and last factor is a shift in the balance between the public and private spheres of life. This is related to the decay of idealism, but is more complex, and harder to pin down.

An important part of what I mean by the 'public sphere' is (or used to be) the local community. I was brought up in a small rural village, which I continued to visit until recently. The village is as populous as ever, but in my lifetime I have witnessed its steady decline as a social organism. At one time, its pulse could be felt in the religious and secular calendar – harvest festivals, village fêtes, and so on. Once, nearly everybody attended such events; now just a few come, mainly middle-aged or elderly, perhaps with some reluctant children in tow.

But the public sphere includes not only the local community, but also all activities based on concerns or interests shared by society as a whole (or at least significant sections of it), activities in which private individuals can come together for common aims. I am thinking of various kinds of voluntary association: churches, political parties, local charitable organizations, and so on.

Our society is by no means lacking in a public sphere, but one of the significant changes in the last few decades has been the relative shrinkage of this side of life, and the corresponding growth in the portion of our existence that is lived in comfortable privacy. Consumer culture emphasizes personal pleasure and convenience. Nowadays we can, if we choose, easily keep ourselves fed and entertained without significant contact with anyone outside the tight circle of the family. Some of the needs that voluntary associations once addressed – the religious ones, for example – now seem irrelevant to many people. And the charitable aims that motivated other associations are increasingly the

71

preserve of professionals and public agencies: they do it better, and in any case, we haven't got the time.

Even the reduced public sphere that remains is partly illusory – a play of images generated by the media, especially television. Soap operas about the intimate communal life in a street or small town substitute for real friendships with neighbours (which perhaps relatively few people now actually experience). Democracy, which should connect us to a public world, mostly boils down to the isolated act of casting a vote, and even this is done mainly on the basis of the media show of election campaigns, with their attendant spin.

The institution of friendship has probably suffered in this process, for the public sphere has traditionally been one of the main arenas for friendship. It provides a context in which people can meet freely on the basis of lasting shared concerns. As such, it is a distinct 'reality', standing apart from both the world of work (where we go, but in many cases rather reluctantly, to make a living) and the purely private world of home and family (where we may find pleasure and affection, but not much scope to fulfil our individual potential, or play a creative role in the world). The waning of the public sphere is also a waning of the context for friendship.

Repairing the net: Buddhism and friendship

Of course, modern life has brought enormous benefits as well as a degree of mutual estrangement. Although the credits in the account have been mainly material, there have also been some gains for the human spirit. For example, in traditional societies, the social group often stifles individuality. The reassuring closeness of traditional life often congeals into suffocation, especially for those who differ from the herd. In the old days, those perceived as odd (in terms of their thinking, values, behaviour, creativity, sexual orientation, or whatever) were often forced into at least the appearance of conformity.

Indeed, it isn't just the exceptional individual who suffers from the oppressive intimacy of traditional life. Children brought up in continual close contact with parents, grandparents, siblings, relations, and neighbours – not finding much solitude – may not develop a strong sense of themselves as individuals. They may therefore never find, in adult life, the autonomy and confidence needed to think new thoughts, or feel anything other than what everyone is supposed to feel. The capacity for independent thought and feeling comes not just from education (crucial though that is) but also from the ability to find a certain distance, both physical and psychological, from the social group. Generally speaking, modern life gives us more chances to find or create that distance than traditional cultures, which have tended to submerge the individual in the group.

So I am not advocating a retreat from socially atomized modernity into an oppressive tradition. The ideal solution to the ills of anomic society would be a middle way between these two extremes – a society that locates individuals within a supportive web of relationships but at the same time allows them to be individuals, or (better still) encourages everyone to *become* an individual, in the best sense of that word.

The Buddha declared his teaching to be the middle way between false and polarized extremes. He used the idea to suggest that spiritual progress is to be found neither in indulgence of the appetites nor in the more extreme forms of self-mortification, but in a sane, moderate discipline of the senses. But the concept of the middle way can also be applied to other things, including the relation of the individual to society as a whole. The Dharma seeks neither to cage us within the close bars of social conventions, nor to set us adrift alone upon the wide sea of anomie. On the one hand, the Buddha conceived of the individual as changing, and potentially changing into something better:

in a word, as evolving. To that extent, his teaching affirms individuality and individual freedom. On the other hand, he taught that kalyāṇa mitratā is the whole of the spiritual life – reminding us that the individual's evolution is only possible in the context of sangha, the network of spiritual friendships.

Even in the midst of anomic society, it is possible (as I know from experience) to find a sangha – a network of genuine friendships based on a shared spiritual ideal. Within such a spiritual community, we can reverse the five conditions I have described as contributing to the decline of friendship in the modern world. To begin with, we can learn from the encouragement and example of others to value friendship properly, and to rid ourselves of limiting views, such as the notion that any warm and intimate friendship must 'really' somehow be sexual, or that the deepest intimacy and warmth can only be found in a sexual relationship.

Within the sangha, we can also experience the kind of friendship that is based on ideals in the fullest sense of the word: the values expressed in the Dharma are not materially redistributive: they urge us to transcend material self-interest rather than just make fair and rational arrangements to satisfy it. At the same time, these ideals are not just 'beliefs', but are embedded in ethical disciplines and spiritual practices that actually change us, and so change our relation to the world. The Dharma's ideals flow from (and lead us towards) a deeper experience of reality. In this way, spiritual friendship is not, as some might imagine, a flight from a tough 'real world' into a consoling private world of personal relationships. Rather, spiritual friendship puts us in touch with the objective reality of our human situation.

A living sangha can do more than help us to transform ourselves in accordance with genuine ideals. It can also equip us with the motivation and the means to work for the benefit of others. A true spiritual community is not an inward-looking 'club', but a compassionate force in the world: it will naturally tend to give rise to institutions and activities through which we can work with friends (much more effectively than we could work on our own) for the good of other people. Accordingly, the more deeply we participate in the sangha, the more we will also find ourselves drawn away from comfortable privacy and towards active participation in the public sphere.

This means that by developing spiritual friendship we are not just doing something for our own happiness, but also making a contribution to reversing the atomization of society. It is more than just a matter of mending our own tiny portion of the torn social net: spiritual friendship helps to re-knit the whole fabric.

This account of the transforming power of friendship is not just a manifesto for what it might do in the future. It closely corresponds to my own experience over the last thirty years. For me, participation in a spiritual community has brought, among other things, a wonderful enhancement of friendship. To be sure, I don't suppose that I would be entirely friendless now if I had never found a sangha. All the same, I can't imagine how any other path might have led me to a life so blessed by such a wide range of friends, or such depth in friendship, as the one I now enjoy.

How can I express something of the way in which spiritual friendship has enriched my life? One aspect of it is freedom from loneliness. Perhaps there is a sense in which our existence can't be absolutely free from loneliness. But I am not speaking now of the existential 'aloneness' that, some say, is intrinsic to the human condition, but of the ordinary loneliness that visits us in varying degrees according to our individual temperament and circumstances (and which seems to haunt us inhabitants of anomic society rather more than it did our forebears). The shadow of this kind of loneliness has progressively lifted from me since I first came into contact with the spiritual community. As the years have gone by, I have come to feel myself linked ever more closely by threads of friendship to that community – and through it to the fabric of humanity as a whole.

From this sense of connectedness has flowed a healthy confidence in myself, a large measure of liberty from the anxiety or insecurity that makes us all doubt our worth from time to time. I feel strongly that I am 'seen', that I am known, am loved, appreciated, and cared for. And because of this confidence, I can inhabit the full range of my being: I can share with friends my deepest or my most fleeting thoughts; I can express myself in my most sombre moods, or at my most frivolously playful.

Then again, I have the great satisfaction of knowing that I am of value to other people in many ways, whether as a confidant to my peers, or as a guide to younger or less experienced friends. In addition to all this, it seems to me that the confidence and clarity I have gained from my friendships has improved the other relationships in my life – with my parents, for example. During the last period of their lives, I was glad to find that I could resolve the minor tensions that had once marred my communication with them, and that we got on better than ever.

I imagine that these human benefits of friendship will easily be intelligible to everyone. Harder to convey, perhaps, except to those who have followed a similar path, is the way in which spiritual friendship has inspired and shaped my spiritual life – has nurtured in me a faith that there is a deeper meaning to existence, and a happy sense that I am leading my life by the light of that meaning. That perhaps is the supreme blessing of spiritual friendship, and one for which I am deeply grateful to all my friends.

Part Two

The Meaning of Spiritual Friendship

5
Friends in the Good

Ordinary and Spiritual Friendship

Someone you like

An advocate in a British courtroom, scoring a point against his adversary (whom he might know slightly) may refer to him as 'my learned friend'. The obituary of a wealthy philanthropist might describe him as a 'friend to the poor'. In order to get discounts on tickets for exhibitions, concerts, or plays, one may enrol oneself as a 'friend' of a certain gallery or theatre. Clearly, 'friend' has a range of meanings, including 'colleague', 'benefactor', and 'subscriber'. Even where the word is used in its basic sense of a warm personal relationship, it does not necessarily imply a very high degree of intimacy.

As the word 'friend' can mean so many different things, perhaps I'd better make clear, before going further, what I take to be its primary meaning. The subject of this book is *spiritual* friendship, but it is difficult to talk about that without first saying something about what friendship means in a more general sense. Once we have made that clear, we can go on to see what spiritual friendship has in common with the ordinary variety, and also how it differs from it. As part of our search for answers to these questions, we will have to venture beyond Buddhist sources. As we have seen, Buddhists in traditional societies never felt much need to discuss what they meant by friendship. Fortunately, though, Western thinkers – from antiquity down to fairly recent historical times – have had quite a lot to say on the subject. In this chapter and the next, let's see what we can learn from Western sources, and how well we can integrate our borrowings into Buddhist thought.

A friend is, according to a typical dictionary definition, someone you know and like. That gives us a good starting point. You cannot make friends with someone who leaves you cold, at least not until your indifference thaws. Pleasure and attraction are essential. Clearly then, friendship is based in feeling. Strictly speaking, it is based in both feeling and emotion, for Buddhist psychology draws an important distinction between these two things: 'feeling' is an automatic reaction to a stimulus, identifying it as pleasant, unpleasant, or neutral; 'emotion' is one's response to that feeling. A pleasant feeling, for instance, usually gives rise to attraction and desire: you will naturally want to prolong or repeat the experience that engendered it. If you enjoy someone's company, you will want to see them again.

The liking felt in friendship is a complex thing that can't be compared to a partiality for a particular food, or a fondness for a pastime. We may enjoy the company of a witty or charming person, yet doubt whether we can trust them. Friendship cannot go very far while that sort of doubt lingers. Friendship thus seems to depend not only on pleasure in the strict sense, but also on a sort of qualitative judgement – a positive valuation of the other person's worth. Samuel Johnson hit the mark when he observed that, for friendship to occur, love must be mixed with 'esteem'.[57]

But this esteem involves more than a judgement of whether the person is trustworthy. After all, we can trust people –

that is, we can feel confident of their good intentions – without necessarily being able to communicate very fully with them: there might be too great a gap in intelligence, emotional maturity, or interests. Of course, every human being is worthy of respect simply as a human being, but the esteem necessary for friendship is much more specific than this: the other person's human capacities must be developed in a way commensurable with your own.

This 'commensurability' need not be tantamount to equality. On this point, I take a broader view than those who regard friendship as by definition a relationship between equals. My experience suggests that strict parity in the here-and-now is not necessary. Nevertheless, friendship does seem to require that the partners respect each other as, in a manner of speaking, serious players in the same game.

The thing that you like and esteem in a particular friend may not be everyone's cup of tea: it might even be ethically questionable. For example, the world's oldest tale of friendship tells of the mythical Sumerian heroes, Gilgamesh and Enkidu – two mighty warriors who fought savagely at their first meeting. They fought so well that they became the best of friends, the fierceness of their struggle guaranteeing the depth of their subsequent respect for one another. The example makes a further point: your most valued friends are those who draw out of you what you most value in yourself. They can do that because they value something similar in themselves: proud warriors befriend proud warriors, poets other poets, horticulturalists their fellow gardeners. Friendship puts down its deepest roots in common concerns, especially those that are not imposed on us by circumstance but spring directly from our own hearts.

Here then we have the foundations of friendship: liking someone, respecting them, having important concerns in common. Yet, essential as they are, these things don't suffice to make someone your friend. Something more is required: your feelings must be returned. Pleasure, respect, and the sense of having common ground must all be mutually felt – something that doesn't happen automatically. They must also be mutually acknowledged, either frankly or tacitly.

We can go further with a little more help from Samuel Johnson – himself a man with a deep appreciation of friendship. Johnson defined a friend as 'one joined to another in mutual benevolence and intimacy' – a definition so good that it survives to this day at the head of the entry for 'friend' in the *Oxford English Dictionary*. If the words 'mutual liking' represent friendship's foundations, then the phrase 'benevolence and intimacy' stands for the edifice itself.

The Latin root *benevolentia* means 'willing what is good' for another person. (*Goodwill* is an exact synonym from the Anglo-Saxon tributary of English.) This is what Buddhism calls *mettā* – a desire for the happiness of others. In everyday speech, when we mention 'love' we usually have in mind an emotion that mixes together the desire to take and the desire to give. Benevolence or mettā corresponds specifically to the latter aspect, and not to the former. It is, to borrow terms coined by C.S. Lewis, 'gift-love' rather than 'need-love'.

Of course, friends are not the only objects of mettā. Because mettā asks for nothing in return, it has an expansive quality that tends towards universality. The more strongly you feel it for this person, the more you are likely to feel it for that person – and for anyone and everyone. Indeed, Buddhism encourages us to feel mettā for *all* living beings, not just friends. But it is easier to feel mettā where we first feel some liking. In a healthy mind, mettā is virtually the reflex of liking someone (although the two feelings are not identical, for liking may consist more of 'need-love' than 'gift-love'). So where mutual liking gives birth to mutual mettā, and where these feelings are strong enough and find opportunity for expression, they may grow into friendship.

True, we may feel mettā for a stranger sitting next to us on a bus, or for people on the other side of the world, glimpsed on television. But such mettā does not lay on us any special obligation to those particular individuals. In contrast, our benevolence for our friends joins us to them (as Johnson put it). It creates a sense of duty. When our friends fall sick, we visit them. If they have financial troubles, we loan or give them money. If they need to talk, we make time to listen sympathetically. Admittedly, we sometimes do such things even for strangers, but in such cases we make a free choice to involve ourselves, whereas with friends that choice has been made beforehand. In short, friendship means that two people feel a responsibility for each other, one that is not imposed from outside but flows from mutual mettā.

There is something else about mettā that we should notice. It is a kind of bridge between ordinary and higher states of consciousness. On the one hand, it is a 'natural' emotion: all human beings experience it spontaneously, even if some only feel it weakly and fleetingly. On the other hand, it is also a 'spiritual' emotion. All spiritual traditions recognize mettā, under one name or another, as a *desideratum*: something required, something to be cultivated as part of the higher life. And in order to maintain mettā steadily, with strength and purity, you have to make a purposeful spiritual effort over many years. Of course, people who make that effort are the exception rather than the rule, so in most human relationships (including most friendships) mettā is mixed with self-interested forms of love.

Still, of the various kinds of relationship that we experience in everyday life, friendship (provided it is not tepid) is probably the one that gives benevolence the most room to develop in a relatively unmixed or pure form. In other affectionate relationships – romantic love, for example, or the closer forms of kinship (our bonds with parents, children, or siblings) – love may be more intense than in the average friendship, but it is also more likely to be coloured by 'need-love', and therefore also more vulnerable to negative emotions such as jealousy and resentment.

Intimacy, the second part of Johnson's definition of friendship, is the fruit of benevolence. A sense of mutual goodwill allows friends to relax with each other. With a friend, you can let down your guard and disclose your real thoughts and feelings. In short, a friend is someone with whom you can (in a significant phrase) 'be yourself'. In his classic essay 'Of Friendship' Sir Francis Bacon described intimacy as a kind of medicine:

> We know diseases of stoppings and suffocations are the most dangerous in the body; and it is not much otherwise in the mind.... No receipt [medicine] openeth the heart, but a true friend, to whom you may impart griefs, joys, fears, hopes, suspicions, counsels, and whatsoever lieth upon the heart to oppress it, in a kind of civil shrift or confession.[58]

Bacon also knew that intimacy is not just an emotional but also an intellectual necessity, not so much because our friends can clarify our thinking for us (although they may) but simply because they give us someone to *think to*. Through communication with a friend, says Bacon, a man comes to know his own mind:

> He tosseth his thoughts more easily; he marshalleth them more orderly; he seeth how they look when they are turned into words; finally, he waxeth wiser than himself; and that more by an hour's discourse than by a day's meditation.[59]

Intimacy requires knowledge as well as feelings. Deep intimacy requires deep knowledge, and that takes time. True friendship is like a tree, taking years to grow to its full height. Candour will speed the growth, but not beyond certain limits, for the knowledge of other people consists in much more than what they can tell you about themselves.

The work of sustaining and deepening intimacy over a long time requires certain qualities of character, especially in the rootless, restless times in which we live. Friendship depends on patience and faithfulness, and for this reason it is, in addition to everything else, a school of virtue. Our important friendships are strands threading the length of the cord of life, helping to imbue it with its proper dignity.

The three kinds of friendship

Thinkers on friendship are sometimes troubled by a moral ambiguity in the subject. On the one hand, most of us probably know intuitively that friendship is connected with what is good in human nature. On the other, it is obvious that in practice friendship does not always go hand in hand with moral goodness. Proverb and example show that there is honour (at least sometimes) even among thieves. Likewise, in the *Sigālaka Sutta*, the Buddha warns Sigālaka of the danger of *bad* friends, which he says are one of the 'six ways of wasting one's substance'.[60] The capacity of friendship to coincide with evil seems to contradict the idea that it has any intrinsic connection with the spiritual life. Why is it that good friends are sometimes bad people? Evidently we have to distinguish between kinds of friendship.

Let's go back to my starting point: friendship is based on liking. But there are various kinds of liking, and each leads to a particular type of friendship. The nature of the liking depends on its object – the aspect that we love in the loved person – for we rarely, if ever, love people in their entirety: we love something in them that is attractive to us. On this point, Western philosophy can contribute something important to our understanding of friendship. Aristotle, in his *Ethics*, distinguishes three things that may attract us in a friend: pleasure, usefulness, and the good. Each of these three things, he says, gives rise to a different kind of friendship.[61]

Those based on pleasure are the ones that correspond closest to everyone's intuitive idea of friendship. We love some friends because we enjoy being with them. Perhaps they are lively, entertaining companions who make us laugh (or better still, laugh at our jokes). They might share with us an interest in jazz, for example, or rock climbing, or politics. Or maybe they just share our opinions, and so give us the pleasant experience of being agreed with. Pleasure-based friendship is a natural and necessary part of human life, for most pleasure is innocent and nobody can do without it entirely. This kind of friendship can be found among all sorts of people, but Aristotle suggests it is especially predominant among the young.

The second category is usefulness (or, more crisply, *use*). We are drawn to certain people because they represent an opportunity to get something we want, and usually we are happy to do something in return. Such friendships, Aristotle suggests, are particularly common among middle-aged and older people. They are often based on common work interests, business deals, political alliances, the exchange of information, and many other practical concerns. For the relationship to count as friendship, the usefulness must be accompanied by genuine reciprocity and goodwill. No doubt there is usually some pleasure involved too, although not enough to sustain the friendship on its own. The 'use' category sounds selfish, but there isn't necessarily anything wrong with it. Everyone has to live, and needs help to do so. Useful friendships are among the social bonds that make possible a peaceful, orderly, and prosperous society.

Pleasure or use, or some combination of both, probably provides the main basis of most friendships. This helps to explain why good friends may sometimes be bad people. Use is always related to some desired end, and ends may be good, evil, or neutral. Some 'useful friends' are honest partners or associates; others are accomplices in crimes or shady deals. Likewise, pleasures may or may not be innocent: some friends enthusiastically play duets or compare computers, but others like to get drunk together, or trade gossip about mutual enemies. Friendships based on use or pleasure may therefore be either wholesome or unwholesome.

In the unwholesome cases, the good aspects of friendship may not disappear altogether, but they inevitably get twisted: qualities such as loyalty, generosity, or courage may all be put at the service of bad ends. If the ends are really bad, this twisting of virtue tends in the long run to destroy it altogether, and perhaps to destroy the friendship too, for benevolence can hardly be dependable where it cohabits with evil.

In addition to pleasure and use, there is, Aristotle says, a third object that can be loved in a friend: goodness. For Aristotle, the good is the proper goal of human life, the fulfilment of all the specifically human possibilities that give dignity to our life. In a nutshell, the good consists of *virtue*.

Nowadays, the word 'virtue' can sound a bit stuffy. To modern ears, it might suggest sexual repression rather than anything more positive. But for Aristotle, the virtuous individual is a happy and noble being, possessed of fine qualities, such as courage, generosity, and friendliness. True, such a 'great-souled man' is indeed self-restrained, because he is ruled by 'the mean' in all things. However, Aristotle's notion of the mean is not an insipid mediocrity, but a balance of opposites, a finely-tuned equilibrium between antithetical traits, each of which becomes unwholesome if given free rein. Courage, for example, is the synthesis of boldness (which flares into foolhardiness if stoked too vigorously) and prudent foresight (which congeals into cowardice if ruminated too long).[62]

But in addition to such qualities of character, virtue – according to Aristotle – also includes 'intellectual virtue', the capacity for a higher mental life, above the appetites and senses – the faculty that opens to man the doorway to a life higher than that of the beasts.

Obviously, Aristotle and the Buddha – neither of whom could have known anything of the other – did not have exactly the same idea about what constituted the good. In Aristotle's view, for example, intellectual virtue is essentially the faculty of reason. Buddhism, in contrast, discerns modes of knowing that are higher than reason. Despite the differences, I think that Aristotle would have recognized kalyāṇa mitratā as one variety of friendship in the good. I also suspect that the Buddha would have agreed with Aristotle's view that there are lower kinds of friendship based on use and pleasure.

This distinction between three kinds of friendship helps us to understand how friendship is always founded on some shared underlying concern, how these concerns can be distinguished from one another, and how we can evaluate them from a spiritual viewpoint. However, we need to apply the idea sensitively. I don't recommend that we start casting a judgemental eye on other people's friendships, pigeon-holing this one as 'pleasure-based', that one as 'useful', and another as 'in the good'. We can't reliably judge the basis of a friendship from outward appearances. This means that friendship in the good cannot be identified exclusively with friendships that are founded on a professed religious or moral ideal. Nor can we directly equate pleasure-based and useful friendships with 'ordinary people's friendships' – and then class the latter as inferior.

No doubt any man or woman who is actuated by a desire for the well-being of others, or by a concern for the truth, is to that extent living from a love of the good, and that motivation is likely to be reflected in his or her friendships. Such people will naturally tend to become friends with others who are similarly 'good-hearted'. Even where moral or religious ideals play little or no part in the life of either person, a friendship might still be tinged with a shared but inarticulate sense of the good. Probably, then, all three elements – use, pleasure, and the good, combined in varying mixes – play a part in most friendships, whether or not they are based on an ideal. Any attempt to classify actual friendships according to the three types would be problematic: most real specimens are probably hybrids.

But where two friends share a conscious orientation to it, the good is more likely to be – or at least to become – the bedrock of their friendship, even though use and pleasure may also play a part. At the very least, such friends will be better equipped to increase the share that the good has in their friendship – better, that is, than those who make no special effort to prioritize the good. So when I speak of friendship in the good, I am thinking on the whole of friendship between those who have – to coin a phrase – 'awoken to the good': that is, people for whom the good is a conscious and important concern.

If we interpret it in this broad way, Aristotle's idea remains useful to our attempt to clarify our understanding of friendship in general and kalyāṇa mitratā in particular. Firstly, we can recognize kalyāṇa mitratā as one variety of friendship in the good. And in doing so we can see how kalyāṇa mitratā is – or certainly can be – a true species within the genus 'friendship', rather than some quite different kind of relationship to which the name 'friendship' has been applied as a metaphor. Secondly, we can understand how, while belonging to the wider genus, it can also differ very significantly from the other species – differ, that is, from those based on use or pleasure, which may be either wholesome or unwholesome.

In addition, we can – if so minded – take up the idea of the three foundations of friendship as a tool with which to understand (and perhaps transform) our personal experience of friendship: each of us can use that tool to discern the part played in our friendships by use, pleasure, and the good – and to nurture the good.

Aspects of friendship in the good

Before we focus on the Buddhist variety – kalyāṇa mitratā – there are a few general aspects of friendship in the good that we need to make a little clearer.

Firstly, how exactly can friendship be 'in' the good? Or to put it another way, in what way can goodness be the foundation for a friendship? It seems to me that there are two possible ways. Firstly, friends in the good are friends because they have something in common: a liking for the good, an attraction to its beauty. The good is the goal they both aspire to, and they sense that they can help each other to attain it. In this way, the good is something 'outside' them – something they go in quest of together, 'shoulder to shoulder'. But secondly, friends in the good also perceive and like the good in each other; so at some moments they stand 'face to face', rather than 'shoulder to shoulder'. Each loves the virtues that are manifest in the other.

Understanding this, we can reconcile two concepts of friendship that otherwise don't seem to mesh – the notion, on the one hand, of friendship as based on a shared concern, and on the other, the idea of loving the friend for his or her own sake – for what he or she intrinsically is. When a friendship is in the good the distinction between these two concepts dissolves.

Perhaps I should add in passing that when I speak of two friends loving each other's virtues, I don't mean to imply that only a saint can be a friend in the good. In one and the same person, virtues may exist side by side with elements of confusion, immaturity, and worldliness. Fundamentally, what one loves most in a friend in the good is that, despite any imperfections, he or she is firmly turned towards the good, and is moving closer to it. It is this fundamental orientation to goodness, rather than any particular quality springing from it, that is the basis of the friendship. One person's love of the good can resonate with the same love in another – even if both also have faults or weaknesses – and from that resonance friendship may be born.

The second topic I want to consider is Aristotle's view that friendship in the good is more 'complete' than the kinds based on use and pleasure.[63] By this, he means that friendship in the good is more than just one sort of friendship among others. He regards it as the best kind – as friendship *par excellence* – because it fulfils his fundamental conception of friendship more perfectly.

I agree with him, inasmuch as I believe that a friendship based on love of the good has the potential to provide a more deeply satisfying form of friendship than the other varieties. When the elements making up friendship – mutual liking, respect, benevolence, and intimacy – stand upon the foundation of the love of the good (rather than on use or pleasure) they stand more securely, and so can rise to a higher level. Here, the liking and respect are based on what is most worthy of liking and respect – goodness. Benevolence, being good itself, is more fully at home here than in other kinds of friendship. And where benevolence is strong, trust can grow, and so intimacy can go deep. In short, friendship in the good seems to satisfy my definition of friendship in a fuller, purer way. Or as Aristotle put it, it is more complete.

But perhaps I'd better guard against misunderstanding. I am not suggesting that a friendship that arises in a formally religious context – between professed Buddhists, let's say – is automatically better than others. We may know other people's religious allegiances – or their lack of any – but on that basis alone we can't say how deeply they love the good, or how far it shapes their friendships. I don't think it is helpful to draw 'class distinctions' in friendships (especially not if we do so in order to pass judgement on somebody else's). However, we may benefit from exploring in depth the implications of a spiritual ideal. In pointing out the special quality of friendship in the good, my aim is to encourage people to seek it out and to nurture it as the relationship that holds out the best hope, in the long run, of fully satisfying the heart.

We have just seen that the completeness of friendship in the good, relative to other kinds, is partly a qualitative thing – the experience of benevolence and intimacy in stronger and purer forms. But it has another important aspect, too – durability. It seems to me that, if we want to experience a long-lasting friendship, the best foundation to choose for it is the good, rather than use or pleasure. Success is not guaranteed (because the outcome will depend on a sustained effort to cultivate the good by both parties) but to the extent that we build a friendship on the good, rather than on some other basis, we have a better chance of achieving an enduring bond. But why should this be so?

Aristotle's answer to this question, like much of his thinking, is based on the distinction between ends and means. He points out that in friendships based on use, the friend is valued not as an end but as a means to something else. When we cease to want that something else, or when we find a better means to it, the friendship loses its *raison d'être*, and is likely to fade away. Pleasure, unlike use, can claim the dignity of being an end in itself, but it is an end that is relative to the individual and his or her situation in life. In other words, what we find pleasant today we may find unpleasant tomorrow, or next year. For that reason, pleasure-based friendships are also vulnerable to decay.

What about the good? The good is an end in itself, but unlike pleasure it has an absolute quality. While a pleasure may seem good today but stale tomorrow, the good is unconditionally good – good not just for certain people at certain times, but good in itself. Virtue, according to Aristotle, tends to endure, and consequently the friendships founded upon it are similarly enduring.[64]

This abstract analysis does seem to correspond roughly to something I have found true – and very important – in experience. In so far as a friendship is in the good, it is based on each person's sense of the inherent worth of their friend, rather than on the friend's capacity to be a pleasant companion or a useful ally in the struggle for some mundane goal. It is also based on a shared sense of what really matters in life as a whole, rather than on the (possibly transient) concerns or desires that one may have during one particular phase of life. To the extent that we really have awoken to the good, we are bound to recognize it as something of abiding importance. That recognition tends to make friendship in the good endure – and indeed to deepen.

From the standpoint of Buddhist doctrine, kalyāṇa mitratā can be understood in much the same way. Buddhism, like Aristotle, also posits an ultimate end, namely enlightenment. And it sees that end not as a matter of personal taste, but as the truest and highest good for all living beings – even for those who as yet know nothing of it. And as I argued in Chapter 2 (in the discussion of Anuruddha and his friends), friendship seems to be one aspect of the enlightened state, and must therefore be counted as part of the end of Buddhism, as well as one of its means.

In practice, of course, things are often more complicated than this. Friends in the good may be sincere in their goodness, but not yet well established in it. They may still be immature in thought and feeling. In short, they may aspire to friendship in the good without yet experiencing it very fully. At this stage, they are quite capable of falling out with each other, and indeed of falling away from the good. It is also possible – especially in our pluralistic modern culture, where many belief-systems compete with one another – to change one's mind about the best route to the good; and such changes are likely to affect one's friendships (although not necessarily to destroy them).

Nevertheless, having acknowledged these ifs and buts, it seems true that friendship in the good – once it has been established between mature individuals – is likely to be long lasting. The deeper and more authentic our commitment to the good, the less likely we are to abandon it – or the friendships we have made in pursuing it. At least, this is implicit within the ideal I have outlined; and – speaking for myself, and those I know intimately – it does seem to be confirmed in experience. In the main, the close friendships I have made in the spiritual life have not only endured, but also deepened – which means that some of them have been going from strength to strength for over thirty years. I notice a similar durability and growth in the friendships of many other people in the spiritual community. But if my description of 'anomic society' (in Chapter 4) was anywhere near the mark, this kind of close and enduring friendship is probably not very common in our culture. In speaking of the strength of my friendships, I hope I don't seem to boast. I only want to bear witness to something that I regard with a grateful sense of good fortune. Any credit is due to my teacher, who taught me to value friendship in the first place, and to the spiritual community he founded.

The final point concerns the compatibility of the three possible bases of friendship – use, pleasure, and the good. The trouble with contrasting friendships in the good with those based on pleasure and use is that it risks making spiritual friendship sound like a rather austere and joyless affair. It isn't, of course. Firstly, although friendship in the good does not depend on ordinary forms of use and pleasure, it can include them. If you have friends in the good, they will certainly help you generously in practical or material matters, and in that sense will be useful. Similarly, such friendships are bound to be pleasurable in many of the ways that any friendship is pleasant: we can share many ordinary pleasures with our spiritual friends.

But secondly, and more fundamentally, the good has use and pleasure in its own right. The kinds of use and pleasure we have been talking about so far are the mundane variety – those that are bound up with the world of the senses (the *kāmaloka* in Buddhist terminology) and with the ego. But in so far as friendship in the good helps us to know the good more deeply, and cultivate it more effectively, we can speak of it as being, in a sublime sense, 'useful'. In addition, friendship in the good has its distinctive pleasure – or rather its proper joy. Admittedly, there may be times when our commitment to the good brings us up against tough challenges in our communication with a friend, and at those times the friendship may not seem so pleasurable. However, if we stick with the good through those challenges, it will stick with us, and in the long run will add far more to the sum of happiness that we find in friendship than to the pain it brings us.

6
The Supreme Mystery

Kalyāṇa Mitratā, Faith, and Wisdom

Forms of friendship in the good

The possibility of friendship in the good exists between two people when each of them has awoken to the good – that is, has made the cultivation of the good a conscious and important concern. But like everything, such friendships can only arise in dependence on specific conditions. In most cases, friendship in the good blossoms out of the fellowship of a group of people who come together because they understand the good in broadly the same way. In other words, spiritual friendship doesn't germinate in just any soil: it needs the seedbed of a spiritual community.

Aristotle himself seems to have developed his ideas of friendship in the good from his experience of something resembling a spiritual community. As a philosopher, he seems a secular figure to us, but his ideal of friendship derived from his experience as a disciple of Plato, and as a member of Plato's Academy in Athens. To the extent that it was dominated by Plato's idealism – his belief, for example, in the immortality of the soul and the existence of an eternal world of ideal forms – the Academy in its heyday must have resembled a spiritual community rather than a modern university. Although Aristotle later moved away from Platonic mysticism, and took much more interest in scientific matters than Plato ever did, his philosophy of man and his ethical ideas remain strongly coloured by the tradition that descended to him from Socrates via Plato. That tradition was spiritual in so far as it emphasized the reflective or contemplative side of life, and gave a central place to truth, goodness, and beauty.

The insight that friendship is intimately connected with the spiritual life is by no means unique to Aristotle. It has appeared in each of the three great spiritual traditions that have been most successful in transcending cultural boundaries: Christianity, Islam, and Buddhism.

In Islam, the ideal of brotherhood between believers, while rooted in the Koran itself, received its classic exposition from the hand of the Iranian al-Ghazālī (1058–1111CE). In his treatise, *The Duties of Brotherhood in Islam*, brotherhood signifies far more than the general obligation of goodwill to one's fellow Muslims. It is, says al-Ghazālī, 'a bond between two persons, like the contract of marriage between two spouses. For just as marriage gives rise to certain duties which must be fulfilled when it is entered into, so does the contract of brotherhood confer upon your brother a certain right touching your property, your person, your tongue and your heart – by way of forgiveness, prayer, sincerity, loyalty, relief and considerateness.'[65]

By a curious coincidence, an ideal of spiritual friendship seems to have flowered in Christianity, quite independently, in the same era. Striking out in a new direction from the earlier, more ambivalent tone of monastic writings on friendship, St Anselm (1033/4–1109), in letters he wrote from his monastery at Bec in Normandy, unfolded a vision of friendship as part of the soul's quest for God. Following in Anselm's footsteps, St Bernard of Clairvaux (1090–1153) also wrote enthusiastically on the subject. But it was left to an English Cistercian monk, Aelred of Rievaulx (1110–1167), to give the theme its fullest statement in his moving treatise 'Spiritual Friendship' (*Spiritualis Amicitia*). Inspired by both the gospel and Cicero's classic *De Amicitia*, Aelred went so far as to make the bold declaration that 'God is friendship'. His book became well known throughout the monastic world in Western Europe, and became popular even among the laity.

As for Buddhism, we have seen how the Buddha declared kalyāṇa mitratā to be the whole of the spiritual life. It is now time for us to look at kalyāṇa mitratā and relate it to the more general idea of friendship in the good unfolded in the last chapter. So far, we have been borrowing a lot of our ideas and terms from Western culture – from writers like Bacon, Johnson, and Aristotle. Those loans were necessary in order to clarify what friendship means, and explain how it is that friendship, which can sometimes be unwholesome, can also be intrinsic to the spiritual life. But can we now attach these ideas securely to the framework of Buddhist thought?

Kalyāṇa and śraddhā

To begin with, what is there in Buddhism that corresponds to 'the good' and 'the love of the good'? In Chapter 1 we saw that 'morally good' is part of the meaning of 'kalyāṇa'. In fact, some translators of Buddhist scriptures routinely translate kalyāṇa as 'good'. Of course, there are other words in Buddhist texts that could be translated as 'good'. For example, there is *kusala*, which is usually rendered as 'skilful', a term that highlights the idea that ethical behaviour requires understanding and intelligence. But the specific connotation of kalyāṇa – as we saw in Chapter 1 – is that the good is beautiful. It is because the good is intrinsically beautiful that we can delight in it and love it, rather than just

rationally approve of it. And that is crucial for friendship because, as we saw in the last chapter, we can only speak of friendship where there is love or liking. For Aristotle, too, friendship in
the good is possible because the good is something that can be
loved, and it can be loved because it is 'fine'.[66] In the original
Greek, the word for 'fine' is *kalos*, which can also be translated as
'beautiful'.

The idea that good actions are beautiful makes sense to
some, but to others it may seem meaningless or sentimental. Perhaps I can anchor the idea in experience by giving an example.
One instance that Aristotle gives of a 'fine' action is the sacrifice of
one's life for others. This puts me in mind of an occasion, years
ago, when I read a newspaper report of a terrible disaster in
which a plane crashed into a river. One man repeatedly dived
underwater into the body of the plane, and in this way rescued
several people. Finally, he dived one more time – and never re-
appeared. Reading the story moved me deeply with an emotion
that seemed to include not only pity but also something else,
harder to define – a sense of reverence, perhaps, or the thrill of
being at once challenged and inspired to live a better life.

Of course, the beauty of goodness is not usually as dramatic
as risking one's life for others. We see it more often in smaller acts
of kindness, courage, patience, or wisdom. But whatever form it
takes, it appeals not to the senses but to some mysterious faculty
of the mind. When we see the good, the world seems set in order
and illuminated. When we want to talk about it, aesthetic experience seems to offer us the closest analogy we can find in the world
of the senses to describe something that is not itself a sense object.
This is why we speak of the good as 'beautiful'.

The capacity to perceive and love the beauty of the good is
a precious human quality. Perhaps it is the most important of
human emotions, and in any case it is certainly something we
need to cherish. I am sure many people shared my response to the
story of the plane crash and that man's sacrifice, but I fear that the

age we live in may be blunting our sense of the beauty of goodness – or, at best, reducing it to a rather faint, sentimental shadow
of itself. Anomic society is not sure what it believes in, apart from
increasing pleasure and comfort for everyone. To pursue the gratification of the senses now seems wholly natural and good, and
even necessary for the economy. Morality has come to mean
keeping that pursuit within certain limits to avoid hurting each
other, or wrecking our health. A sort of prudent hedonism is the
tacit philosophy of consumer culture. From this viewpoint, the
good often seems to have been reduced to a necessary but rather
dull set of rules – almost the opposite of whatever lends pleasure,
excitement, and charm to life. How can that be 'beautiful'?
Prudent hedonism can't make much sense of a man who keeps
diving into a submerged aeroplane, repeatedly risking his life for
others until he finally loses it.

But if we can speak of the good as beautiful, we should not
forget that it is also *true*. Sense-beauty may lead us into delusion,
but the beauty of the good is grounded in reality. For Buddhism,
virtue is based on an intuition of the way things really are, not on
a hopeful fantasy of how they ought to be. According to the
Dharma, a principle of ethical balance is somehow built into our
existence, no matter how monstrous the world may be on the surface. Whenever the Buddha wanted to explain what he meant by
'right view', he mentioned, among other things, faith in karma –
the teaching that we can escape neither the painful consequences
of our evil acts nor the happy consequences of our good ones.
From the Buddhist viewpoint, those who perceive this truth –
whether by intuition, self-knowledge, or observation of the lives
of others – are more in tune with reality than those who do not.

For Buddhism, the good is therefore not simply the good
but rather the true-good-beautiful – or, in one word, the kalyāṇa.
This is why the Buddhist scriptures say that the Dharma – which
instructs us in the way things are and how to live in harmony

with that reality – is kalyāṇa in its beginning, its middle, and its end.

Our sense of the kalyāṇa is natural – it is a faculty that we all possess to some degree. The capacity to discern and love the good is part of what makes us human. Admittedly, the faculty is not equally developed in everyone, but anyone can cultivate it, just as anyone can learn to appreciate beauty in other forms, such as art, music, or poetry.

Does Buddhism have a name for this faculty that loves the good? If we can name it, we will also have named the liking that is the foundation for kalyāṇa mitratā. Buddhist scriptures don't directly answer this question, but they do provide us with the materials for an answer. They frequently speak of a mental state called *śraddhā*.[67] Here again we meet a term for which no single English word is really adequate as a translation (which is why I generally use the Sanskrit word). 'Faith' is probably the least unsatisfactory equivalent, provided we remember that this kind of faith is not belief in something for which we have no evidence.

But if not blind belief, what does faith mean in Buddhism? Summarizing a range of traditional teachings, we could say that śraddhā is a name for what happens when a rational-intuitive grasp of what is true (faith in realities) leads to an appreciation of what is morally and spiritually good (faith in qualities). This in turn leads to a desire to realize those qualities in oneself, coupled with a confidence that this is possible (faith in capacities – i.e. one's own). These three dimensions of śraddhā are sometimes called 'conviction', 'lucidity', and 'longing', and they seem to correlate respectively with the truth, the goodness, and the beauty of the kalyāṇa.

Śraddhā is of fundamental importance in Buddhism. It is the foundation of the whole spiritual life, the motivating force that inspires us to start living that life – and to keep living it until we have attained its goals. Although the Buddhist scriptures themselves don't directly link śraddhā with the adjective 'kalyāṇa', or explicitly speak of it as the basis of kalyāṇa mitratā, to do so requires very little extrapolation. For example, in some versions of the *Abhidharma* (a systematic account of the Buddha's teachings on the mind) śraddhā is said to be present in any wholesome mental state, and this seems tantamount to saying that śraddhā is the basis of the human emotional response to the good. In the Buddha's discourses, śraddhā is usually mentioned as the attitude that one should cultivate towards the Three Jewels – the Buddha, his Dharma (or teaching) and the Sangha (meaning here the *ārya* sangha, or enlightened community). Without doubt, the Buddha and the Sangha are, for a Buddhist, the highest embodiments of the moral and spiritual qualities that are elsewhere described as kalyāṇa. As for the Dharma, we have already seen that the scriptures more than once describe it as kalyāṇa in every part.

The fact that most scriptural references to śraddhā relate it to the Three Jewels should not mislead us into thinking that śraddhā is the name for an emotion that Buddhists must uniquely reserve for the Three Jewels (in the way that, in the theistic faiths, some believers might say that 'worship' is due only to God). True, the Three Jewels – including the enlightened Sangha – are the ideal objects of śraddhā in the sense that they are the highest ones (and also the most dependable). They are like mountains appearing over the horizon – the fixed points that we have in view as our goal, no matter from which direction we may approach them. But this does not mean that the Three Jewels are the *only* possible or fitting objects of śraddhā. Indispensable as they are to our sense of direction, we cannot fix our eyes on the distant mountains alone, and ignore our immediate surroundings. In the same way, we need śraddhā for the spiritual friends who are our guides and companions in the here and now, as well as for the Buddha and the great Buddhist teachers of the past.

Indeed, the śraddhā that we feel for our actual spiritual friends is arguably of more immediate practical importance than the higher (but for most of us, largely theoretical) śraddhā for the enlightened Sangha. As the great Tibetan Buddhist teacher Gampopa pointed out, there is a sense in which our greatest bene-factors are the 'ordinary human beings' who become our spiritual friends at the beginning of our spiritual career. Such unenlight-ened friends (who nevertheless sincerely strive for the kalyāṇa) can help us to set our feet on the path, whereon we will eventu-ally encounter wiser ones.[68]

If we understand kalyāṇa mitratā to be based on śraddhā, we can see that the love that Buddhists feel for their spiritual friends is of fundamentally the same nature or tendency as the love that they feel for their highest ideals – the Three Jewels – rather than a subjective partiality that they should perhaps give up at some future time when they have 'gone beyond' it. This puts me in mind of a story about the friendship of Sāriputta and Ānanda, retold in a book about the Buddha's great disciples:

> *Whenever Ānanda received choice robes or other requisites he would offer them to Sāriputta, and in the same way, Sāriputta passed on to Ānanda any special offerings that were made to him.... The subcommentary says that later teachers commented on this: 'There may be those who say: "We can well understand that Ānanda, who had not yet attained to arahantship, felt such affec-tion. But how is it in the case of Sāriputta, who was a canker-free arahant?" To this we answer: "Sāriputta's affection was not one of worldly attachment, but a love for Ānanda's virtues (guṇa-bhatti)."'*[69]

Before we leave the subject, there are a few more things we need to appreciate about śraddhā and its role in spiritual friendship.

Firstly, śraddhā belongs to the Buddhist vocabulary of mind: it is, to begin with, a mental state. But it is not content to remain one: its nature is to express itself in action. In Buddhism, śraddhā is what leads one to 'go for refuge' to the Three Jewels: that is, to commit oneself wholeheartedly to the Buddhist path.

Going for refuge is often thought of as a sort of preliminary statement of intent or a declaration of allegiance, but it is really much more than that. Buddhists recite the verbal formula of going for refuge again and again throughout their lives. For many, no doubt, this is no more than a cultural convention, but the real purpose of the words is to express and strengthen something far deeper – the emotional force that impels the mind towards the goal of enlightenment. In other words, the act of going for refuge is what happens when śraddhā is strong enough to determine the direction of one's life. It is śraddhā in action.[70] In this sense, it is not śraddhā alone but the focusing and expression of śraddhā through the act of going for refuge that is the basis of all spiritual friendship in Buddhism.

Perhaps I should guard against a misunderstanding. We should not confuse the love that produces spiritual friendship – the resonance that exists between two people who both go for refuge to the Three Jewels – with the sort of group loyalty that we might feel to others who think and behave in the same way as we do. Of course, this sort of generalized fellow feeling can be found in Buddhism as much as elsewhere, but it is not what I mean by spiritual friendship, which is a relationship between individuals. For kalyāṇa mitratā to develop between two people, each must actually witness the other's going for refuge, and love it.

Finally, it is important to remember that the act of going for refuge is not done once and for all, but is repeated, at deeper and deeper levels, throughout one's spiritual life. The Buddha said that progress in his Dharma came only gradually, just as the ocean deepens gradually with distance from the shore. Going for refuge is cumulative, and therefore so is kalyāṇa mitratā. As our connection with the kalyāṇa strengthens, our friendships in the kalyāṇa will likewise become stronger and deeper.

Friendship and wisdom

Translated into Buddhist terms, 'friendship in the good' becomes friendship based on śraddhā – friendship that flows from the love of the kalyāṇa. But there was another important idea that we borrowed from Aristotle, namely that such friendship in the good is an end in itself, not just a means to something else. Actually, we had already touched on this point in Chapter 2, when I retold some of the scriptural stories of friendship between the Buddha's enlightened disciples. I suggested that we could only understand the friendship between Sāriputta and Moggallāna, or between Anuruddha, Nandiya, and Kimbila, as an aspect of their enlightened state.

This idea has a deep meaning for me. I am not satisfied with any conception of spiritual friendship that sees it just as a rung on the ladder to enlightenment, or even as the whole ladder (as that still implies that the ladder can be kicked away when one gets to the top). I feel that kalyāṇa mitratā can reach a stage at which it actually becomes the very experience of self-transcendence that is the goal of Buddhist practice. Spiritual friendship can, in a sense, become enlightenment. To make such a big claim for it may seem bold and unorthodox. How can it be fitted into the framework of the Dharma?

As a first step towards answering that question, we need to consider what we mean by 'enlightenment'. To be sure, enlightenment transcends anything that we might say about it, but Buddhist tradition has nevertheless spoken of it in a number of ways. One of the most important of these is that enlightenment is the overcoming of the delusion of self. As unenlightened humans, we all divide the world into self and not-self, sharply separating what is 'in here' from what is 'out there'. This dichotomy of subject and object is the most fundamental pattern in our feeling and thinking, yet Buddhism teaches that it is a delusion, something not really present in our experience but imposed on it by our mind.

The delusion of self is not just a harmless fancy. It causes us a lot of pain. By organizing our lives around it, we create suffering – sometimes for others, and more or less constantly for ourselves. For example, we spend our time and energy in chasing pleasant experiences to gratify the 'self' and keep it happy, or in building high walls of comfort and security around it in an attempt to screen it from the winds of change. In all our struggles, we find no real peace and no deep satisfaction. To be sure, things sometimes go well, and life seems to assuage our desires, or appease our fears; but sooner or later they reappear in new forms. Buddhism teaches that the vain belief in a self is not just one cause among others, but the primal cause of all our suffering – the engine that drives us round and round on the wheel of birth and death. Conversely, to see through the delusion of self is what sets us free from that wheel. That 'seeing through' is the function of transcendental wisdom (prajñā), and wisdom is the essence of enlightenment.

The main expression of the subject–object dichotomy in everyday life is the fact that each of us is preoccupied with looking after number one. In the abstract, we know that other people are centres of consciousness, desire, and suffering, like us. However, we easily lose sight of that, especially when we are gripped by such emotions as desire or anger or fear. At such times, other people seem to stand 'out there' in relation to our own impulses: we see them as either aids or hindrances to our aims, as either pleasant or unpleasant; or perhaps simply as irrelevant, and therefore as objects of our indifference.

In practising the Dharma, we try to be aware – and not to forget, even at moments of crisis – that other people are subjects too. Bit by bit, we develop our capacity to let go our preoccupation with our own subjectivity, and instead to empathize and identify ever more strongly with others. This leads us ultimately to the insight that the whole notion of a world composed of independent 'subjects' and 'objects' is not in accordance with reality. In this way, wisdom arises. Wisdom is not utterly foreign to us even now. Some reflection of it illuminates our experience at moments. Any of us, in moments of sympathy, can identify with other people, putting ourselves in their shoes. The task of the spiritual life is to create such moments deliberately, and to make them longer.

At this point, we can begin to discern a relationship between wisdom and friendship. As we have seen, one of the basic ingredients of any friendship is benevolence – what Buddhism calls mettā. It is impossible to imagine how there could be a genuine, deep benevolence except on the basis of those moments in which we step outside ourselves and identify with another person. Mettā therefore already has something of the flavour of wisdom in it. Unlike most forms of love, it is a strangely objective emotion, because it is free of appetite or anxious dependence, and therefore is not clouded by subjective concerns. By calling mettā objective I am not suggesting it is in any way cool or cerebral: it is as warm and vibrant as any other form of love. But unlike other forms, its nature is to appreciate others for what they are in themselves, rather than as sources of satisfaction of one's own desires. Mettā is therefore an emotion that carries you out of yourself, transporting you beyond self-concern to identification with another human being. Of course, in order to take you very far outside yourself, and for more than a short while, mettā needs to have a strength it can find only in sustained spiritual practice.

Perhaps mettā on its own – at least if we define it as an emotion, without any thinking aspect – may not break down our delusive belief in the distinction between self and other, but our capacity for mettā, if we develop it far enough, stretches and attenuates that belief to the point where it can be 'seen through'. We should therefore conjoin our efforts to feel mettā with an attempt to cultivate wisdom – recognizing that, in a way, these are just two different aspects of the same process.

One method of doing so is to adopt the self of another person as one's own – that is, to give it equal or even preferential treatment. This means making an effort to be mindful of that person in a very sustained and sensitive way: to resonate deeply with their point of view, to identify with their needs and wishes, whether in large matters or small, to give priority to their happiness and well being, even where doing so obliges one to put aside one's own desires.

The great Buddhist poet Śāntideva expressed this idea beautifully in his poem, the *Bodhicaryāvatāra*:

> *Through habituation, there is the understanding of 'I' regarding the drops of sperm and blood of two other people, even though there is in fact no such thing.... Why can I not accept another's body as my self in the same way?... In the same way that, with practice, the idea of a self arose towards this, one's own body, though it is without a self, with practice will not the same idea of a self develop towards others too?... Whoever longs to rescue quickly both himself and others should practise the supreme mystery: exchange of self and other.... All those who suffer in the world do so because of their desire for their own happiness. All those happy in the world are so because of their desire for the happiness of others.... For one who fails to exchange his own happiness for the suffering of others, Buddhahood is certainly impossible.... Therefore, in order to allay my own suffering and to allay the suffering of others, I devote myself to others and accept them as myself.[71]*

The capacity to identify with others is thus no less than an attack on the root delusion of selfhood. It is the overthrow of prudent hedonism: by exchanging one's own happiness (that is, pleasure and comfort) for the suffering of others, one reaches the supreme happiness of enlightenment. From the viewpoint of everyday common sense, of course, this is a very peculiar notion. No wonder Śāntideva called it the supreme mystery.

Śāntideva makes it clear that one must ultimately practise this exchange of self and other in relation to all beings. But that leaves the question of how and where to start. One can hardly hope to go straight to the ultimate stage. Common sense suggests that, until we can practise it in relation to a few people – or at least one – we can have little hope of doing it indiscriminately for the infinite number of living beings.

But who should those few, or that one, be? Mettā is the basis of the exchange, so it would seem logical to start where one already feels a strong benevolence. It would also seem wise to choose somebody for whom one's mettā is pure – that is, not too mixed with one's own 'need-love'. Where our own needs are involved – especially the need to be loved and valued by someone else – it is easy to delude ourselves that we are giving selflessly, when in fact we are not. Before we can effectively practise the exchange of self and other, we need to know the nature of our love. Otherwise the practice could be a plunge into a subtle form of selfishness – one from which we may emerge feeling cheated when the loved one fails to keep his or her part of the bargain. However, if the love is genuinely based on the kalyāṇa, we won't expect the loved one to do anything in return for our giving up of self. A mature spiritual friendship therefore seems to be the best context in which to practise the exchange of self and other.

What does this high-sounding ideal mean in daily life? We can start to practise the exchange of self and other simply by being more and more mindful of the needs of our friends, and putting them before our own. Whenever one makes some kind of sacrifice, or gives up something for the sake of a friend, one takes another small step forward on the path of transcending self: one enters more deeply into the friend's subjectivity and lets go attachment to one's own. In Anuruddha's words, 'Why should I not set aside what I wish to do, and do what these venerable ones wish to do?'[72]

Eventually, this practice may lead to the insight that the whole notion of subject and object is just a useful manner of speaking, not a metaphysical fact. Once that insight has arisen, it will tend to spread outwards, leading us to identify not just with present friends, but with all living beings, and not just in flashes but as a habitual mode of consciousness.

Here perhaps is another aspect of the Buddha's saying that friendship is the whole of the spiritual life: it gives us a context in which to practise selflessness. Indeed, it can be not just a context for that practice, but a form of it. And for Buddhism, selflessness – in the sense of realizing the truth of *anātman* (or 'not self') and so living for the sake of others – is the ultimate goal of all spiritual practice.

7
A Second Self

The Benefits of Friendship

In this section, so far, I've been discussing spiritual friendship in analytical terms – clarifying its meaning and examining the way it relates to some of the central ideas of Buddhism. I hope the result of this exploration is that we can now see how spiritual friendship can truly be friendship (in the usual sense of the word) and also 'spiritual'.

But a philosophical analysis of this kind doesn't reveal much of what spiritual friendship looks like from the inside. To redress the balance, I now want to make kalyāṇa mitratā more tangible: to say something of what it means in experience, and to suggest some of the many ways in which can enrich life. Hence, in this chapter, I am going to talk about the benefits of spiritual friendship.

'Benefits', in this case, does not mean perks. The rewards I have in mind are not external things added on to spiritual friendship. In a sense, the benefits of kalyāṇa mitratā *are* kalyāṇa mitratā. They are the tangible expressions of the śraddhā and mettā that flow between two people and make them friends with one another.

Broadly speaking, the benefits of friendship are of three kinds: practical, psychological, and spiritual. Although my subject is kalyāṇa mitratā, I don't want to imply that such friendship offers only austerely 'spiritual' rewards and not the other kinds. In fact, spiritual friendship – being, as Aristotle put it, more complete than those based on use and pleasure – is likely to bring us practical and psychological benefits in correspondingly ampler measure. So, to draw a rounded picture, I will say something about all three types of benefit.

Practical benefits

In his discourse to the young layman Sigālaka, the Buddha had quite a lot to say about the practical benefits of friendship. Among other things, the *Sigālaka Sutta* gives us a brief but quite well rounded picture of how, in the Buddha's view, close friends take care of each other. As we might expect, a big part of this is material aid. For example, one characteristic of 'the helpful friend' is that 'when some business is to be done, he lets you have twice what you ask for' (presumably because he knows that, in order not to trouble him too much, you have understated your real need).

The sutta also points out the value of friendship for mutual protection in an indifferent or dangerous world: friends are said to look after you and your possessions 'when you are inattentive'. The medieval commentary (which unfortunately doesn't always go very deep) interprets 'inattentive' as 'drunk'! But I suspect the Buddha was thinking more broadly than that. His words point to the fact that nobody can be constantly alert to all dangers or opportunities of life, and one of the advantages of intimate friendship is that a friend's awareness can supplement one's own. For example, a close friend checks that you have your glasses (knowing how often you forget them), or keeps an eye on your house while you are away, or shows you the ad you failed to notice, describing a job that would suit you down to the ground.

Even such humble, everyday favours hint at the extension of selfhood to another person – a distant foreshadowing of the exchange of self and other. And in fact the Buddha plainly tells Sigālaka that a man should minister to a friend by 'treating him like himself'. A good friend is a second self, someone who identifies with you through all your ups and downs, sharing your life's difficulties and dangers as well as its pleasures and successes. Such a friend, says the Buddha, is 'a refuge when (one) is afraid' – someone who risks danger for your sake when everyone else shuts the door in your face.

The sutta points to various other benefits, too. One is that a friend defends your reputation, and so protects your position in society: he 'stops others who speak against you' and 'commends others who speak in praise of you'. To do that, a friend must identify with you even in your absence. Sigālaka also learns that true friends 'show concern for your children'. This presents an important and challenging idea – that to love one's friends means to care not only for them but also for those they care for.[73]

In the *Sigālaka Sutta*, the Buddha sheds a lot of light on the benefits that friendship brings to the individual. Nowadays, having learned to think of human beings not just as individuals but also as part of a complex, ever-changing social organism, we can raise a further question: does friendship also bring any practical benefits to society as a whole?

Very probably it does. For example, friendship is likely to be an important factor in the cohesion and vitality of social institutions. Power and money alone cannot ensure the success of institutions: no organization can thrive when personal relations between its members turn cold. Armies have long known the value of *esprit de corps*, and nowadays even private corporations are learning the importance of a positive 'corporate culture' and 'team skills' – which are really just dilute forms of friendship.

Friendship is likely to be particularly important in the work of idealistic organizations such as charities. This is because ideals cannot, in the last analysis, be reduced to abstract propositions. Ideals are elusive, for they are intrinsic to the *being* of the individual. They are seen as much in the way people act as in what they profess. The success of institutions based on ideals therefore depends on the extent to which those ideals are enthusiastically shared by the staff. But such sharing cannot be accomplished once and for all; it requires constant renewal. No doubt things like mission statements and seminars can help, but probably not much if the 'corporate culture' lacks a spirit of cooperation and harmony. If I am right in regarding ideals as intrinsic to personal being, it follows that they can be fully communicated only in friendship. Consequently, idealistic institutions will thrive to the extent that there is friendship within them.

Psychological benefits

The primary psychological benefit of friendship is that it assuages loneliness. The prolonged experience of loneliness with no prospect of relief is perhaps one of the most painful things that a human being can endure. It is significant that in oppressive regimes the torturers often rely as much on isolation as on pain to break the will of dissenters.

Speaking personally, one of my most painful memories is of a time in my teens when my schoolmates systematically ignored me. For some reason, I became a sort of black sheep for a few months, and nobody wanted to be seen with me. It was a boarding school and my family was far away, so there was no escape from the isolation. Every day I had to walk about three-quarters of a mile from my boarding house to the school. I will always remember the dreadful moment each morning when I left the house and saw everyone else walking down the road in pairs or small groups, chatting freely, while I had to walk alone. Quite often, nobody really spoke to me for several days at a time.

The strangest effect was that I started to lose my sense of identity. I don't mean that I forgot my name or my past, but I did lose some of the *feeling* of who I was. Fortunately, the boycott ended, as mysteriously as it had begun, and once again I found myself part of the herd.

In hindsight, the experience suggests to me how our normal sense of self arises from interaction with people. Much of our being, although we think of it as 'inside' us, is continuously created through social life. The process goes on even in our most casual and superficial interactions with others, but with friends it happens more powerfully and deeply. Friends are always telling us, 'You're OK,' even if they don't usually say it in words. A good friend is a kind of mirror in which you can see your own face, and feel pleased to see it.

Traditional societies knew less of loneliness than we do. The *Sigālaka Sutta* says nothing of it, but it does refer briefly to a related psychological benefit of friendship: a good friend 'tells you his secrets' and 'guards your secrets'. Friends give us opportunities for self-disclosure, the release of the inner pressure of thoughts or feelings that we need to express. As we saw in Chapter 5, Sir Francis Bacon called this 'a kind of civil shrift': that is, a form of confession outside the framework of religion or ethical judgement.

At several moments in my life, I have found myself listening to people telling me things that have weighed heavily on their minds for years, perhaps since childhood: long-hidden urges, fears, or feelings of guilt. I know that some of those people felt as if the act of self-disclosure brought them back into the human race after a long exile. When these revelations included a confession of wrongdoing, the matter usually didn't seem very serious to me;

but in some cases it had assumed monstrous proportions in that person's mind, just through having been bottled up so long. Counsellors and psychotherapists provide valuable help to many people, but I suspect that much of it would be unnecessary if the institution of friendship were in better health.

When we hear the words 'self-disclosure', we tend to think first of the release of painful emotions, such as shame, anxiety, or grief. But the human heart also needs to express its hopes, joys, and enthusiasms. Lovers, in real life as well as in song and story, always want to tell the world that they are in love. All of us have at some time tried to share some experience of beauty or significance, only to be deflated by obvious signs of incomprehension or indifference in a listener's face. Too many experiences of that sort can make us stifle what is most vital in our own hearts.

But at its highest, self-disclosure becomes something more than revealing secrets, or giving vent to moods. We need someone who can see and draw out who we are, or rather who we are becoming. Each of us has an inner world, full of thoughts and feelings that are amorphous or embryonic: we can only give them their proper shape through communication. Whenever we succeed in communicating them, we are changed, becoming someone new. Our best friends, the ones who care about us and understand us deeply, are creative listeners, partners in our act of self-creation. They are not spectators at the unveiling of a statue, but midwives helping us to bring something – ourselves, in fact – into the world.

This is why we may sometimes feel strangely lonely with those who love us, if their love affirms us in a general way but misses the deeper dimensions of our being. One's parents, for example, usually care deeply for one's health and worldly success, but may show little recognition of one's spiritual needs. Similar problems can occur with friends from earlier phases of one's life. They can understand who we used to be, but cannot help deliver the new self that is trying to be born. We need friends with whom we can achieve a measure of 'self-actualization'.

The best kind of friend is therefore someone who, to coin a phrase, helps you to unravel yourself to yourself. This may (or may not) include a quasi-psychoanalytic exploration of your unconscious, but actually the most important kind of unravelling is to do with your understanding of life and what matters most in it: an exploration that is, in a sense, more philosophical than psychological. This is the deepest part of what one is missing when one feels lonely – a recognition of oneself as an individual with a unique, unfolding mind. A friend who gives us such recognition is precious indeed. Sadly, many people never experience this kind of friendship.

Clearly, the psychological benefits of friendship are enormous. As we saw in Chapter 5, Sir Francis Bacon compared a friend to a medicine that cures 'stoppages and suffocations'. This is suggestive, but it doesn't go far enough. We should not think of friendship only as a remedy, to be taken in doses sufficient to relieve the congestion of unexpressed emotions, or dull the ache of loneliness, and then returned to the psychological first-aid kit. It is more fundamental to human existence than that. Loneliness is the absence of friendship, in the same way that darkness is the absence of light, or suffocation the absence of air, not vice versa.

Spiritual benefits: the exchange of the kalyāṇa

Spiritual friendship includes all the practical and psychological benefits that are found in ordinary friendship, and adds its own special varieties. The exact nature of these depends on the kind of spiritual friendship in question: vertical or horizontal. And in fact, the vertical category really comprises two sub-categories, for the partners are spiritually unequal, and the benefits therefore differ depending on which side the relationship is viewed from.

On one side is the 'aspiring friend': that is, the less experienced one, who aspires to a fuller experience of the kalyāṇa. On the other side is the mature friend: the one who is riper in the kalyāṇa. (We have to remember that the terms are relative, for the same individual could be in both categories at the same time, in relation to different friends.)

We have already looked at the benefits that an aspiring friend can gain from a mature one. In effect, that is what we learned from the discussion in Chapter 1 on the five conditions for the liberation of the heart. In the present chapter, I want to discuss the other two categories: the benefits of horizontal friendship and the benefits that the mature may gain from the aspiring friend.

Firstly, then, let's consider the benefits of horizontal friendship. Many Buddhists think of spiritual friendship almost exclusively in terms of a teacher–disciple relationship. Those who enjoy intimate day-to-day contact with their spiritual teacher may not feel they are missing much if they lack peer friends. However, I suspect that even someone in such a fortunate (and rare!) situation could still benefit from more attention to horizontal friendship.

My own experience has taught me that a small circle of equals, enjoying intimate friendship with one another, can aid each other's progress greatly, provided they also have some contact – a little may be enough – with more mature friends. This idea is explicit in the story of Anuruddha and his friends, each of whom felt it was 'a great gain' to be living with the other two. If one has enough contact with peer friends, a mutual 'exchange of the kalyāṇa' will tend to occur.

One part of this exchange is that friends can help us stay afloat in the troughs of our going for refuge. Anyone who has taken up spiritual practice in earnest knows that it isn't easy: one often feels tempted to give up the struggle and live an ordinary life. You may, for example, lose confidence in your ability to meditate. You may find yourself wistfully thinking about little luxuries or career opportunities you have given up to live the spiritual life, and wondering if you made the right choice. More seriously, you may have doubts about the tradition you are following, or even about the Dharma itself. Worst of all, you may feel disappointed or disillusioned with many of your fellow practitioners, or your teacher. In the midst of such storms, the love that you feel for a trusted friend may be the only thing that keeps you going till you reach harbour again.

Aside from such crises, just being around spiritual friends constantly nourishes the part of you that loves the kalyāṇa. Conversely, if you spend too much time with people who have no interest in spiritual life, your own feeling for it will tend to fade, and your whole spiritual ideal may start to seem unreal, a castle in the air.

The other aspect of the exchange of the kalyāṇa is to do with *apatrāpya*, a concept introduced in Chapter 1. *Apatrāpya* is a kind of ethical osmosis by which you absorb the moral sense of your spiritual friends. This benefit comes more obviously from one's mature friends. Nevertheless, peer friends can also play a big part in it: in some ethical matters, they will be more sensitive than you are, just as you will be more acute than them in others. Also, since your peer friends have more frequent contact with you, they will be much more aware of your ethical blind spots than your mature friends (with whom, in an unfeigned way, you will tend to be at your best). Your peers can help you to overcome such blind spots, partly by example and partly by gently pointing out your faults to you. They can also help you by hearing your confessions – a subject I will discuss in Chapter 10.

Spiritual benefits: how the wise grow wiser

Does the mature friend gain any benefit from contact with the aspiring friend? Or is it just a chore, however conscientiously undertaken?

There can certainly be pleasure in association with aspiring friends. After years of practising the Dharma, it is refreshing to rediscover in a less experienced (and usually younger) friend one's own first attraction to the kalyāṇa. New beginnings, such as dawn or spring, evoke in everyone a sense of wonder and hope, and a replenishment of energy. Likewise, contact with the vigorous, uncompromising idealism of youth is delightful, bringing a renewal of one's own zest.

But we can go further. Aristotle said that a good man needs friends in order to benefit them.[74] Intrinsic to goodness is the thirst to do good, and friends, being nearest, are naturally among the first objects of that desire. But if this really is a *need*, then we have to say that the good man's friends benefit him too, by satisfying one of his needs. In vertical kalyāṇa mitratā, the mature friend fulfils his or her need to do good by nurturing and educating the spiritual impulse of the aspiring friend.

In Mahāyāna Buddhism, friendship is an important channel for the bodhisattva's work of leading all beings to enlightenment. We glimpse this in the *Gaṇḍavyūha Sūtra*, when Mañjuśrī singles out the young Sudhana for attention and encouragement.[75] Such friendship cannot be a chore, for according to Mahāyāna teaching, the bodhisattvas experience their 'work' as play (*līla*, in Sanskrit). Naturally, bodhisattvas spend a lot of time on things other than friendship, such as meditation, worship of the Buddhas, and teaching large assemblies. But I find it hard to conceive of a bodhisattva with no friends – one that never communicates the Dharma deeply in the context of a personal relationship.

So the aspiring friend offers the mature friend refreshment and a nurturing task that is fulfilling. But surely the aspiring friend, having nothing to teach, cannot actually help the mature friend to make further spiritual progress? We can't be so sure. Perhaps the mature friend can find in the relationship something like the self-actualization that we saw to be one of the psychological benefits of ordinary friendship. In trying to share insights with a less mature friend (who can't easily grasp those insights intuitively) one is forced to articulate them more fully and precisely. In this way, the volatile understanding acquired through spiritual practice is manifested and perhaps 'fixed' – like a photographic image after the developing process. The insights are thus revealed in sharper lines and brighter colours, and so may become the basis for further and deeper insights. Friendship, as Sir Francis Bacon said, is the means by which a man 'waxeth wiser than himself'.

In this way, an aspiring friend can be a midwife to a mature friend's wisdom, despite not being his or her equal. In Chapter 5 I suggested that the necessary basis for friendship is not strict equality but commensurability. When two people recognize each other as engaged in essentially the same project – as with two practitioners at different stages of the same spiritual path – they can be friends, even if separated by a wide difference in degree.

Perhaps even Buddhas – to take the ultimate example – only acquire their full Buddhahood in the act of communicating the Dharma. Communication is intrinsic to human nature, and the notion that this communicative dimension of consciousness is (or even can be) absent from enlightenment seems to me too narrow a conception of the enlightened state. We have to think of the human communicative faculty not as being abolished at enlightenment, but as transformed and refined. What is more, this aspect of consciousness cannot be wholly satisfied with superficial or general modes of communication: it requires scope for continuity, depth, and specificity. In a word, it requires friendship.

Let's consider the example of the most famous 'aspiring friend' in the scriptures. Ānanda, it seems, was not the most talented of the Buddha's disciples. Indeed, tradition has saddled him with a reputation for some major gaffes (such as failing to take the 'broad hint' that he should urge the Buddha to use his power to extend his own lifespan, rather than renounce the life principle at the age of eighty).[76] Nevertheless, Ānanda seems to have been second to none in his enthusiasm to hear the Dharma. He insisted, for example, that the Buddha repeat to him any discourses delivered in his absence. Ānanda was not just devoted to the Buddha as a person, but was also endlessly receptive to his spiritual genius. One of the best blessings that a creative mind can find is an enthusiastic and appreciative listener, who fans the creative fire in which such a mind finds its fulfilment. No wonder the Buddha found Ānanda the most satisfactory of his personal attendants, and kept him on in that role.

Perhaps it would be going too far to say that the Buddha 'needed' Ānanda: no doubt he would have been blissful in his enlightenment with or without his faithful attendant. But it is possible to think that the benefits in the friendship were not all on Ānanda's side. And if that were the case, the Buddha must have found such benefits not just with Ānanda, but also with other disciples with whom he enjoyed a close relationship, such as Sāriputta and Moggallāna.

And perhaps not just with human friends. One of the epithets commonly attached to the Buddha is 'teacher of gods and humans'. When he withdrew into solitary meditation, he was not necessarily alone: according to some scriptures, he sometimes entertained visitors from the heavenly realms, whose nocturnal arrival was signalled by mysterious lights in his vicinity. Those who prefer a strictly rational and down-to-earth Buddhism are free to regard these tales as superstitious accretions, or perhaps as a kind of psychological allegory. But it might be that the Buddha needed friendship with beings at a more refined level of existence in order to communicate insights too subtle for human ears.

Spiritual benefits: sheltering the flame of the Dharma

Friendship brings spiritual benefits not only to individuals but also to the world as a whole, as it plays a crucial role in the preservation and transmission of the Dharma.

Earlier, in discussing the practical benefits of friendship, I suggested that it helps social institutions to sustain and communicate their ideals. Similarly, membership of a spiritual community means something more than 'signing up' with others to a list of abstract propositions. It means participation in a common spirit; and this spirit can be adequately experienced only in friendship. Through the medium of the sangha, the Dharma is perpetuated as a living force from one generation to another. In this way, today's spiritual friendships benefit those not yet born.

It is only through the sangha that the Dharma can survive as something more than words on paper, or an institutional shell. The sociology of religion speaks of a phenomenon called the 'routinization of charisma'. This means that the followers of a charismatic religious teacher usually attempt, after the founder's death, to perpetuate their cohesion and purpose by codifying a doctrine, formulating rules, and founding institutions. This process is probably necessary, yet how often, in the history of religious movements, it seems to contribute to the loss of something vital but intangible in the founder's vision.

The most striking historical example I know is the rapid rise and equally rapid 'routinization' of the Franciscan order within the Roman Catholic Church. The order, inspired by the leadership and example of St Francis himself, grew very swiftly in his lifetime. Not long after his death, however, a conflict flared up between two wings of the order: the 'Spirituals', who wanted to adhere to the pure vision of Francis, and the 'Conventuals', who wanted to establish the Franciscans on the same lines as the other monastic orders of the day. The conflict ended in the triumph of the Conventuals and – tragically – the persecution of some of the Spirituals.

The bitterness of the struggle seems to show that Francis was unable to transmit fully the gentle and loving quality of his own vision. The most likely explanation of the failure is that his order grew too fast for his inspiration to be properly shared. His influence could not be absorbed and transmitted through such a rapidly expanding body.

Perhaps the lesson to be learned from this story is that a spiritual community can only expand at the speed at which a circle of friendships can grow, otherwise it becomes merely an institution. To be sure, an institution may still be a force for good in the world. It may still be animated here and there, and from time to time, with flashes of the original fire. But an institution is something less than a spiritual community: a mere institution lacks the spiritual community's harmonious unity – the state of being 'one in mind' – and its vitality.

I am not saying that institutions are necessarily the enemy of harmony or vitality. Actually, they are indispensable if a spiritual group wishes to grow beyond a small, private circle, and to influence the world. But institutional growth should ideally be the servant of an expanding network of friends, rather than a substitute for it.

It follows that one measure – perhaps the best – of the spiritual vitality of a religious group or institution is the strength of spiritual friendship among its members. If they are connected to one another in a web of friendships, and if they attach a high value to those friendships, it augurs well for their survival as a true spiritual community. Equally auspicious would be signs that, as well as getting on well with each other, the members are friendly to people beyond their own charmed circle. Spiritual friendship is not exclusive and is always eager to make new friends.

Part Three

Spiritual Friendship in Practice

8
Elective Affinities
Choosing Spiritual Friends

Universal love or 'particular friendship'?

Choice is implicit in friendship. Of the billions of human beings in the world, only a few can become one's friends. Seeing this, some conclude that friendship is at best irrelevant and perhaps an obstacle to the spiritual life, which aims at impartial love. The particularity of friendship is, on this view, incompatible with the grand universality of Buddhist compassion or Christian charity.

I think this idea is mistaken, but it is influential. Even a distinguished thinker like Schopenhauer (who prized friendship highly) could write that

> *Friendship is only limitation and partiality; it is the restriction to one individual of what is the due of all mankind, namely, the recognition that a man's own nature and that of mankind are identical. At most it is a compromise between this recognition and selfishness.*[77]

Spiritual friendship has often been beset with such suspicions. In the Christian tradition, it flowered for a while in the high Middle Ages, receiving the blessing of Saints Anselm and Bernard, and the eloquent advocacy of Aelred of Rievaulx in his influential treatise *Spiritualis Amicitia*. Yet this renaissance of classical friendship in the new context of Christian monasticism had to overcome resistance: certain elements of the Rule of Saint Benedict were unfavourable to personal friendship, or at least could be applied in such a way. Permission to speak, for example, was controlled by Superiors, whom the Rule urged seldom to give it. At the same time, a perceived need to prevent 'faction' (a potential threat to the unity of the monastery) sometimes made monastic authorities suspicious of strong personal loyalties among the monks. And the fear of homosexuality, which was regarded as a grievous sin, probably also worked against close personal friendships. Although the pro-friendship views of Anselm, Bernard, and Aelred made headway against this culture for a while, the same anxieties – that friendship was divisive, or a temptation to carnal sin – resurfaced in the later Middle Ages and eventually grew so strong that, according to one authority, 'friendships of any sort were banned from the cloister'.[78]

Some Buddhists, too, reject the idea that friendship is part, let alone the whole, of the spiritual life. To them, it is at best irrelevant and at worst contrary to the spirit of Buddhism. 'It is a form of attachment,' they say. And as we have seen, there are Buddhist texts that appear, on a superficial reading, to lend support to their view.

To me, the idea that friendship is somehow contrary to the spiritual life has always seemed a misunderstanding – the product, perhaps, of an asceticism that has taken a wrong turning. As far back as I can remember, my intuitions have supported the idea that friendship elevates and enriches life, and that whatever humanity's highest possibilities may be, friendship must in some way be part of them. My practice of the Dharma over the years has generally confirmed those intuitions. Experience and observation have shown me that friendship tends to produce an enlargement rather than a restriction of one's sympathy for humanity as a whole. Through a sustained and deepening experience of friendship, we learn to trust other people and ourselves more fully. It helps us to heal our psychological sore spots, and to open defensive barriers that were previously locked tightly in place. As a result, we relax and gain confidence, and start to take a more positive, sympathetic, and forgiving view of our fellow creatures in general.

Hence I don't agree with the idea that friendship – and least of all kalyāṇa mitratā – is 'limitation and partiality'. I don't think such a view is sustainable when (in the way outlined in the last few chapters) we understand friendship as a bond based on mettā and śraddhā.

Mettā, or benevolence, is both universal and particular. It naturally develops into friendship whenever it can. Of course, that development is only possible in certain conditions, namely when two people feel it mutually, when their minds and capacities are developed to a commensurable degree, and when circumstances permit the growth of intimacy between them. Friendship is thus one of the fruits of mettā – something that grows when mettā finds the right soil and climate – and not a limitation of it.

Perhaps we can grasp this idea more clearly through an image. Mettā is like a pyramid resting on a vast base (all beings) but reaching up to a pinnacle of a few intimate relationships. This suggests how the universal and particular dimensions of mettā don't contradict one another, but harmonize with – and even require – each other. The particular must be squarely founded upon the universal, as the summit of the pyramid rests on its base. In other words, without a background of universal goodwill, friendship tends to be exclusive and cosy, a closed circle or sphere. Conversely, the universal must rise to the particular: without friendship, goodwill is likely to be more theoretical than real, shying away from depth and obligation – a flat, featureless plain, with no pyramid in sight.

Spiritual friendship rests not only on mettā, but also – and in a sense even more fundamentally – on śraddhā. All friendship involves choice, because it is always based on liking. This is equally true of spiritual friendship, which is based on a special kind of liking. Śraddhā is a discriminating love: it does not draw the heart to everyone equally, but only to those who love the kalyāṇa. Nevertheless, the friendship that develops from śraddhā enhances the heart's love for *all* beings.

A compromise is something that dilutes each of the things that share in it. With due respect to Schopenhauer, friendship, and particularly spiritual friendship, cannot rightly be understood as a 'compromise' of universal love. We don't usually think of a bridge, for example, as a compromise between the two banks of a river, or a stairway as a compromise between two storeys of a house.

Approaches to choice

In ordinary life, the choice of friends is usually rather unconscious: most ordinary friendships just happen, impelled by mutual liking between two people, without much thought on either side. This does not mean that there has been no choice, only that the choice has been made cumulatively, through numerous small actions. When we make friends in this way, we don't usually reflect on how the new friendship will affect the rest of our life. But spiritual friendship cannot be quite like this. The Dharma teaches us to imbue all we do with awareness – to recognize the emotional roots of our actions, and the place to which they are likely to lead us – and this naturally extends to our choice of friends.

Few people have a worked-out theory of friendship, but everyone has some view of what it is, however inarticulate. I have noticed that when people become enthusiastic about the idea of spiritual friendship, they sometimes approach it almost romantically at first, assuming that their choice of friends should be based on strong, spontaneous feelings, and trusting that first impressions are reliable.

It is true that, occasionally, deep and lasting friendships develop swiftly and with a sense of inevitability. For example, the essayist Montaigne – one of the great writers on friendship – believed that 'some inexplicable force of destiny' mediated his friendship with Etienne de la Boétie. However, he also believed that their bond was so rare that it would be 'something if Fortune can achieve it once in three centuries'.[79] One would therefore be unwise to wait for such a 'decree of heaven' in one's own case.

Actually, what I call the romantic approach is often the enemy of real friendship. The fact is that we are always falling in love (or in hate) just a little. I am not speaking of sexual feelings, but of the liking and disliking that constantly arise as we interact with others. We are usually too immersed in this to see it clearly. However, as one becomes more mindful of one's feelings and thoughts, one discovers a constantly shifting magnetic field of attraction and aversion towards other people.

You might notice this whenever you find yourself among a new group of people – when attending a course or a conference, for example, or mixing with new companions on a holiday. It is an interesting exercise to keep track of one's changing responses to such new acquaintances, and observe how one feels alternately drawn towards and repelled by them, trying to decide whether to like them or not. The lesson to be learned is that such feelings are superficial: they arise and die quickly, like waves breaking on a beach. Unless you have unusual intuitive abilities, your initial like or dislike of someone won't be a reliable guide to his or her potential as a friend. In marriage, whirlwind romances often lead to early divorces, and the same principle applies in friendship.

Spiritual friendship is natural and spontaneous, but that does not mean it manifests immediately, at the first meeting. It is more likely that your appreciation of the kalyāṇa in another person will develop gradually. The qualities that are initially attractive are those lying on the surface of the personality, such as charm, wit, or easy warmth. But the qualities that make a spiritual friend – for example honesty, courage, faithfulness, or patience – only become visible slowly. It is surprising how often people who initially find each other boring or annoying eventually become very good friends.

The main basis for choosing a spiritual friend is that you sense that he or she loves the kalyāṇa, and you feel an attraction to that. By 'attraction' I mean a heartfelt response, not just a detached, abstract recognition that 'this is a good person'. Only this heartfelt response provides a base for spiritual friendship; other forms of attraction depend on outward things that make people useful or pleasant. All the same, it's worth taking a little time to see whether prospective friends can actually live from their love of the kalyāṇa. In other words, do they consistently keep up the effort to develop spiritually, and know how to make that effort effectively?

The second thing to consider in choosing spiritual friends is practicality. One part of this is checking that the potential friend is not so committed to other friendships that he or she simply does not have the time for a new close connection. The other aspect is simple proximity – living near one another. Frequent personal contact is vital to getting a close friendship going. Later on, it may be possible to maintain it even while living far apart, but it is very difficult to *start* a friendship at long distance.

A convergence of interests (other than the Dharma) may be relevant in choosing spiritual friends, but less so than you might think. Some interests – a shared love of the arts, for example – can create opportunities for friends to help and encourage each other in refining their awareness. But such things may or may not be connected with the kalyāṇa; to the extent they are detached from it, they won't enhance spiritual friendship.

The main factors in choosing spiritual friends are therefore simply seeing that they go for refuge to the Three Jewels, loving that, and having ample opportunity to be with them. Are there no other criteria to add to the list? I can only think of one: it is probably better to choose friends who do not share one's weaknesses, as this would undermine the 'exchange of the kalyāṇa'. Someone who tends to be passive, for example, or short-tempered, or prone to depression, might do well not to choose somebody with exactly the same tendency.

Friendship is not something to go into lightly, especially if (as I will recommend later) the friends are going to commit themselves to deepening their friendship. Some people, newly enthusiastic about spiritual friendship, make such a commitment without quite realizing what it implies. Later, when problems arise, they may back away, and that can sometimes cause both parties to feel hurt and reluctant to try again. It is good to bear in mind that, in embarking on a spiritual friendship, we are starting something that, if it comes to fruition, will last the rest of our life. The relationship will bring with it obligations, and will probably require us to come to terms with some of our own foibles, as well as our friend's. The choice of friends is therefore something that is worth taking time over.

The pyramid of friendship

Each of us needs a range of friends. It contradicts the non-exclusive spirit of friendship to concentrate wholly on one person. It is unwise too, as a reliance on one person may make that relationship too heavily loaded with all one's needs for intimacy. An unhealthy attachment can then easily build up, which may later flip over into tension and conflict. On the other hand, some people may tend to spread themselves rather thinly over a wide range of acquaintances, not finding much real depth in any one friendship. How can we find the middle way between these extremes?

I said earlier that a pyramid is a good symbol of the synthesis of universality and particularity in mettā. It is also one possible image for the ideal balance between range and depth in friendship. Let's explore this symbol, bearing in mind that what follows is meant to be suggestive, not prescriptive.

In terms of the pyramid image, personal friendships would comprise the top few levels of the structure. At the summit would be a few very strong friendships, characterized by the deep intimacy that comes from spending a lot of time together over many years. A friend in this category is someone who is often in your thoughts, even when he or she is not around. Each such friend is potentially a 'second self' – someone with whom you can practise what Śāntideva calls 'the exchange of self and other'.

Just below the summit would be a wider tier, made up of warm friendships, rather less intimate than those at the summit, but perhaps only because of circumstance. The friends in this band could eventually be at the apex of the pyramid. They are people that you actively maintain contact with – perhaps through an occasional walk in the park, a lunch, or a phone call. Most of them probably live not too far away from you, so it is easy to keep in touch.

The next tier down comprises a wide range of cordial acquaintances. Some of these friends may live a long way from you. You don't keep up with them so actively, and they do not come into your thoughts so often, but whenever a situation (such as a larger gathering of the spiritual community) brings you together with them, you are glad to have the chance to catch up.

Further down the pyramid are all the people that you meet casually, and whom you treat as potential friends (that is, with warmth, interest, and sympathy). Beyond that, the pyramid extends, widening, towards infinity: you think of all living beings, visible or invisible, with friendliness.

The pyramid has ascending stairways on every side: people can always move up higher. Naturally, the upper tiers of the pyramid tend to get more crowded as life goes on! Fortunately, however, they have an amazing capacity to expand to make room for new arrivals. This is partly because, once a deep friendship has been formed, it can be sustained with less face-to-face contact than is required at first. This fact allows old friendships to be maintained in spite of physical separation, and also leaves open the possibility for new significant friendships at every stage of life.

Helpful as it is, the pyramid image has a weakness: it does not illustrate the balance of vertical and horizontal friendships.

For most people, horizontal friendships naturally tend to be more numerous. Through them, we integrate ourselves into the sangha at the outset, and they support us psychologically and spiritually as we become more committed, and as we perhaps start to take some responsibility within the spiritual community. They also help us to round out our development through the exchange of the kalyāṇa.

Obviously, though, the upper tiers of the pyramid should also include some mature friends – those we recognize as going for refuge more deeply than we do, and who are more experienced in the spiritual life. These will probably be less numerous than our peers, but we will need at least a few in the early and middle stages of our spiritual life. Later on, new friendships of this type are less likely to appear.

Once we have been following the spiritual path for some years, and have gained a measure of depth and experience ourselves, it is also good to have among our closer friends at least one or two who are *less* experienced than we are. (If one's work is the communication of the Dharma, this may become the largest category.) This is spiritually valuable, not just for them but also for us, because they help us to strengthen the kalyāṇa in ourselves by sharing it with others.

Friendship and the sexes

One question that arises in choosing spiritual friends is whether the friend's sex makes any difference. In traditional societies, of course, this was never an issue: social mores prescribed that friendship was, virtually by definition, a same-sex relationship. But the line that used to divide the worlds of men and women has now largely been erased. Most of us are educated in co-educational schools, and very few occupations are still sexually segregated. In their leisure pursuits, men and women mingle freely.

The breakdown of the social barriers between the sexes extends to the realm of personal friendship. For one thing, many people today regard their spouse or lover as their best friend. Apart from that, many people have close friends of the opposite sex. In fact, there are women who actually prefer men as friends, and vice versa. Like so much else, the roles and social behaviour of men and women have changed a lot in the last hundred years. And as the changes have largely been for the better, is there any reason now to assume, in the old way, that we are going to find our best friends from among our own gender?

Perhaps not, but it seems to me that things are more complicated than this – at least in the case of kalyāṇa mitratā, and probably in the other kinds of friendship too. Probably the best way I can explain why I think this is by recounting some personal history.

In the early days of the Buddhist order I belong to (i.e. in the late 1960s and early 1970s), most of our activities – our retreats, for example – mixed the sexes together, in keeping with the spirit of the times. But gradually, many of us – both men and women – came to notice something that contradicted our initial expectations. To our surprise, we seemed to get more fully into our spiritual lives when we got away from the other sex for periods of time. When we did so, we found that our meditation went better, that we became inwardly calmer and less distracted, and that we felt more inspired to practise the Dharma. Above all, we learned that kalyāṇa mitratā unfolded more easily and went deeper with friends of our own sex. There was a certain transparency in communication, a depth of mutual understanding, a freedom from subtle tensions – and consequently a relaxation and intimacy.

Not that we all decided to become monks or nuns. Far from it: although few of us were married at that time, nearly all were very young – and enthusiastic about the sexual revolution then taking place. Nor did the men and women in our order abandon friendships with one another, although the new idea did seem to demand some changes in the way we interacted with each other – a learning process that was awkward at times. We therefore remained involved with the opposite sex as lovers or as friends. Nevertheless, we found that our spiritual life benefited a lot if we spent a significant portion of our time in the company of spiritual friends of our own sex.

One part of the explanation for this is fairly obvious, and very much in keeping with traditional Buddhist teaching. Most people find it easier to put aside the distraction of sexual desire when they get away from the opposite sex for a while. Situations that help us to relinquish sexual thoughts are valuable aids to calming the mind and cultivating *dhyāna*, the bright, serene state of consciousness that we can find in meditation.

But this doesn't seem adequate as an explanation. After all, for some Dharma practitioners – older ones, for example – sexual craving isn't necessarily a big distraction. And, of course, a significant minority of people are physically attracted to their own sex, and logically one might expect them to find single-sex situations potentially even more distracting than mixed ones. But in practice we discovered that such personal factors didn't make a lot of difference. The idea didn't just work for 'straights' or for young people awash with hormones. Male or female, gay or straight, young or old – most of us seemed to gain a lot from spending time in single-sex environments. It seemed to give us access to something more positive than just a temporary respite from sexual desire. It brought a release from some subtle psychological tension and allowed our communication with one another to become more authentic. And spiritual friendship seemed to grow best in the soil of that relaxed, transparent fellowship.

Evidently, our new approach was based on something more than the avoidance of sexual craving. But what was that 'something more'?

One aspect of it was the discovery that in the company of trusted friends of our own sex, we could express ourselves in a more rounded way. Men, for example, no longer felt obliged to appear quite so stoically immune to emotional hurt or fear. Conversely, women were more able to express themselves forthrightly without worrying about whether that might make them look 'unfeminine' in the eyes of men. With friends of our own sex, we could explore wavelengths of our psychological spectrum that we automatically toned down when members of the other sex were around. Through that exploration, we became more truly ourselves, and achieved a deeper intimacy with one another.

But something else was going on – something more elusive but perhaps even more important. It seemed as if, when we spent time with spiritual friends of our own sex, we could communicate with one another in ways that were more firmly based on śraddhā – the love of the kalyāṇa. When we stood on the terrain of same-sex friendship the compass of śraddhā usually pointed north, but in the company of the other sex, the needle could swing around confusingly.

So what magnetic fields were at work? One of them, at least, was easy to identify: many of us recognized in ourselves a tendency to idealize the other sex (not en masse, but those to whom we felt some kind of attraction) and to mistake our idealized images for the kalyāṇa. To be sure, one can put all sorts of people on pedestals, not just members of the opposite sex. But the opposite sex does seem to be one of the most tempting targets for naive projections of the good and beautiful. Perhaps this is because we can't help perceiving the opposite sex as 'other' in a fundamental way; and those who seem 'other' can easily become a screen on which we cast the image of what we long for. Between men and women, of course, such projections are particularly associated with falling in love, but they also arise in other, subtler forms, not necessarily linked to erotic feeling.

While we were discovering these things within our spiritual community, most of us were unaware of other people carrying out similar explorations. But elsewhere, at roughly the same time, feminist women who felt misused by men, or by a male-dominated culture, were starting to rally together in support groups, and learning that same-sex friendships helped them to emerge as individuals, to build confidence and find their voices. And by the late 1980s the luminaries of the emerging 'men's movement' – Robert Bly and others – were leading men on a similar journey. So, as it turned out, we weren't alone in our discovery of the value of same-sex friendships. Or perhaps I should say '*re-*discovery', for in former eras, such friendships seem to have been an important part of life for more or less everyone.

In speaking *for* the positive advantages of friendship with our own sex, I am not speaking *against* friendship between men and women. That would be absurd (not to say rather hypocritical, as I have close women friends). Although there are factors that complicate communication between the sexes, there is also, of course, a fundamental human solidarity that goes beyond those factors. Any friendship – irrespective of the friend's sex – is precious, something to be cherished.

I only want to suggest that it makes sense, in trying to build kalyāṇa mitratā, to focus our efforts on our own sex. That doesn't oblige us to avoid the friendships that often spring up spontaneously between men and women. Nor does it mean that we shouldn't actively seek friends of the opposite sex if we feel inclined to do so. Indeed, friendship between the sexes probably has its own special lessons to teach us. However, I suspect we will only be able to learn those lessons when we have a range of friends – including some very close ones – of our own sex.

9

The More Loving One

Building Spiritual Friendships

Spiritual friendship as a practice

Aristotle said that 'Friendship seems to consist more in loving than in being loved.'[80] The implication is that friendship is something that we *do* rather than a state we passively inhabit, and that does seem to me the truth of the matter. Kalyāṇa mitratā doesn't come to us automatically just because we are intellectually convinced of its value, or because we keep the company of like-minded others. We need actively to pursue and cultivate it.

The last chapter offered some principles to guide us in our choice of spiritual friends, but once we have chosen, the task of actually building the friendship still lies ahead. In the remaining chapters of this book, I intend to explore the nature of that task.

To call it a task is not to imply that spiritual friendship need be laborious, nor to deny the importance of spontaneity. Kalyāṇa mitratā arises from a vital and authentic feeling, the spark of a mutual attraction to the kalyāṇa. But that spark will not necessarily ignite a steady fire unless it is carefully tended. To

build a deep and enduring friendship requires not only spontaneous feeling – crucial though that is – but also the application of
some intelligent effort. As I hope the next few chapters will show,
the essential nature of that effort is to persist in relating to one's
friends by deeds of friendliness in body, speech, and mind.

We can understand this by analogy with meditation. One
of the traditional Buddhist words for meditation is *bhāvanā*,
which literally means 'making become'. Viewed as *bhāvanā*, meditation consists of the active cultivation of wholesome mental
states. *Bhāvanā* isn't the whole story: meditation also has a receptive dimension – it involves opening up or attuning ourselves to
currents that are already flowing within our consciousness. But
the active or creative dimension of meditation is equally important. Indeed, although both aspects are probably necessary
throughout the spiritual life, I suspect that in its earlier phases
most of us need to put rather more emphasis on the active side.
The same is true in spiritual friendship: there, just as much as in
meditation, we need not only to attune and respond, but also to
initiate, to nurture, and to work patiently to overcome hindrances.

If we rely too much on spontaneous feelings – as in the
'romantic' attitude to friendship that I described in the last chapter – we may not get very far in building kalyāna mitratā. Any
deep friendship is likely to require us to come to terms with those
aspects of the other person that we find uncongenial, or even
annoying. We won't be able to do that without making some
effort. It is rather like learning to live in another country. At first,
we will probably be charmed by the novelty of our surroundings,
but then we may go through a long period of irritable frustration
with local customs: the food tastes funny, the shops open at odd
hours, and the voltage is different. Eventually, though, if we stick
with it, we adjust and come to feel that we have gained a second
homeland. Building a friendship is rather similar, for every
human being is another country. That, of course, is why they are
so fascinating – and why getting to know and love them can be so

rewarding – provided one doesn't too quickly give up, pack one's bags, and go home.

Of course, it takes two. The effort must be reciprocal. If only one of the parties is making it, then the relationship hardly deserves the name of 'friendship'. Nevertheless, I think that the wise approach to friendship is to try to put the accent on giving rather than taking. If we do that, we are quite likely to find that, in the long run, our own emotional needs also get deeply satisfied. Two lines from the poet W.H. Auden sum up the ideal attitude:

If equal affection cannot be,
Let the more loving one be me.[81]

Spiritual friendship, while undoubtedly a joy, is therefore also a practice. As such, it has a challenging, objective element: other people – even our spiritual friends – simply will not always do what we want them to do, or be what we want them to be. They are intractably themselves, defying our mastery, so we have to come to terms with their individuality, and enter into that individuality by the exercise of our powers of imagination and empathy.

Spiritual friendship is best regarded as a slow-growing perennial. It may not blossom much in its first year or two. When we look back over the history of our friendships, we are likely to find that our best friends are those we have known longest, or the ones in whose company we have shared important experiences or tasks, or those with whom we have worked through the tensions that arise in any intimate human relationship. The very closest bonds are likely to be those that involve some combination of all these elements.

The value of commitment

As we saw in Chapter 5, there can be no friendship without mutual acknowledgement of liking. Such acknowledgement may be implicit – not directly avowed, but amply shown through attention, appreciation, or kindness. And that may be enough. Nevertheless, there is a lot to be said in favour of the explicit acknowledgement of friendship. If kalyāṇa mitratā is the whole of the spiritual life, it doesn't seem altogether wise to found such an important thing on tacit assumptions. In their direct, unself-conscious way, children often say to each other, 'I like you. Can we be friends?' Grown-ups may prefer to put it in more sophisti-cated words, but in essence we need to say the same thing.

If acknowledgement is the first step in cementing friend-ship, the next is commitment. In our spiritual friendships – or at least, in a few really important ones – we need to have a sense that we are creating bonds that will last a lifetime, not just provisional associations that we can freely leave behind when our interests change, or when difficulties arise. Without this attitude, we are unlikely to find much continuity and depth in kalyāṇa mitratā.

But if we are looking for continuity and depth, we will want to be sure that at least some of our prospective friends are looking for the same things; otherwise we run the risk of disappointment and wasted time. This is why an explicit mutual commitment can be valuable in our main friendships. As I have said, a lot of effort may be needed to overcome the challenges and difficulties of forming spiritual friendships, and that effort is much more likely to be sustained if the friends have pledged themselves to it.

In this area, Buddhists could perhaps learn something from the Islamic tradition. From the early days of Islam, the principle of cementing a friendship through public commitment was enshrined in the tradition of the 'contract of brotherhood'. The eleventh-century scholar and Sufi, al-Ghazālī, discussed this sub-ject in his treatise *The Duties of Brotherhood in Islam*. He took the practical view that, at the beginning of a friendship, the two friends should be clear about how far they want their friendship to go in terms of mutual obligation, and should even work out a 'contract' to specify their duties to each other.

How odd that seems from our viewpoint today! Yet to me there has always been something attractive in the idea. My friend Sona and I put it into practice when we first became friends in the 1970s. We decided, for example, to give each other access to all our material possessions, and each of us became a signatory on the other's bank account. In addition (as Sona was planning to leave the country to work overseas for a few years, while I was to remain in England) our contract included provisions to sustain the friendship during this separation. For example, we agreed to call one another to mind every day in the *mettā bhāvanā* meditation practice (the 'cultivation of friendliness'), and to write to each other regularly.

Sona and I have honoured our contract: we have remained very close friends for some thirty years now – a time-span that has included substantial periods of working and living together, as well as long periods when our paths have diverged. At the moment we are again working together, and the two of us are sharing a house with other spiritual friends. When we are both at home, Sona and I meet for at least a short time every day to exchange confessions, discuss our meditation, and talk over anything that is on our minds. It would be difficult to exaggerate the value of this relaxed, intimate daily exchange to my spiritual life.

Of course, I have other important friends with whom I have never made such an explicit contract. Nevertheless, I find my friendship with Sona has a special strength and depth, and I think that comes, at least in part, from our original explicit agreement: it provided a foundation that has allowed the friendship to grow, and has sustained it through the separations and tensions that are bound to beset any relationship.

I know that for many people today the idea of a contract of friendship will seem a peculiar notion, and at first sight perhaps not an appealing one. In our socially atomized world, we have got into the habit of limiting our obligations and keeping our options open. For us, mobility is part of our ongoing quest for personal fulfilment. We are always 'moving on' in one way or another – to a better job, for example, or a bigger house, or a nicer neighbourhood. As a result, we may tend – perhaps not as a conscious policy, but by a kind of self-protective instinct – to hold back from investing too much in personal ties of friendship, for to do so would set limits to our mobility. No doubt some degree of this kind of flexibility is an inevitable feature of modern life. To my mind, though, something vitally human is lost if we let the principle of 'open options' colonize every department of our life.

I think it can be helpful to express one's commitment to a really important spiritual friend through some kind of ceremony. In the order to which I belong, we have established an optional ceremony for cementing important 'vertical' friendships. This has proved very effective. Perhaps in time we will have a similar ceremony for 'horizontal' friendships. That would not be any great novelty: publicly recognized and ceremonially sealed peer friendships once existed in many traditional cultures.

In modern life, ceremony plays a more limited role than in traditional cultures, and we often don't feel wholly at ease with it. Nevertheless, ceremony can play a very valuable part in life by making important but intangible things (such as relationships or the major transitions in life) more visible and hence more 'real'. Significant developments in the way that individuals relate to each other or to the wider group need to be made explicit. Only then do they become facts, rather than vague perceptions, subject to doubt, dispute, and reinterpretation. Ceremony is at least one effective way to invest these elusive things with the solidity that they must have if we want to build on them.

Of course, before entering into a firm commitment to a friendship (whether or not that commitment is to be expressed ceremonially) one should make a realistic appraisal of one's capacity to honour it. Keeping up a substantial but purely voluntary obligation requires a strong character. To make a commitment to something that exceeds one's present capacity may actually set back one's spiritual growth, for the knowledge that we have reneged on a commitment tends to weaken our self-respect and confidence. While not timorously underestimating ourselves, we also have to be shrewd judges of our present limits.

Time together

Spiritual friendship is based on sharing a love for the kalyāna with another person, and seeing the kalyāna in that person. But to see deeply into the good qualities of other people is a gradual task. It requires the two prospective friends to spend a lot of time together. The point may seem obvious, yet I find that many people don't quite appreciate the extent to which long and close acquaintance is needed before we can really know another human being. The Buddha himself thought it worthwhile to spell this out in some detail to King Pasenadi:

> It is by living together with someone, great king, that his virtue is to be known, and that after a long time, not after a short time; by one who is attentive, not by one who is inattentive; by one who is wise, not by a dullard.
>
> It is by dealing with someone, great king, that his honesty is to be known, and that after a long time, not after a short time,...
>
> It is in adversities, great king, that a person's fortitude is to be known, and that after a long time, not after a short time,...
>
> It is by discussion with someone, great king, that his wisdom is to be known, and that after a long time, not after a short time; by one who is attentive, not by one who is inattentive; by one who is wise, not by a dullard.[82]

In a nutshell, the Buddha was saying that it takes time and a lot of communication to get to know someone in depth. This raises the question of how best to arrange our lives to make time for kalyāna mitratā. To pose that question is to open up the large and complex subject of lifestyle, but I will touch only briefly on it here, as I have discussed it extensively elsewhere.[83]

Spiritual friendship is not something that requires us to follow any one particular way of life. For each of us, the optimum choice of lifestyle depends on our individual temperament and circumstances. Among my Buddhist friends and acquaintances, for example, there is a wide spectrum of lifestyles. Some people live communally, as I do. Others live alone or with a spouse or partner (with whom they may be raising a family). In their work, too, they are very diverse. Some work together to teach Buddhism or run Buddhist enterprises, but many follow more conventional occupations. But despite this outward diversity, I am sure that the overwhelming majority of them, whatever their lifestyle, would say that they value spiritual friendship highly, and have at least some significant experience of it.

From temperament and long habit, I myself love the communal lifestyle and my work for the Dharma. I find that, among its other advantages, this way of life creates ample opportunities for developing spiritual friendship. But I am well aware that it doesn't suit everyone and that it is also possible to thrive spiritually – and enjoy strong spiritual friendships – while living in other ways.

Those who don't feel drawn to the communal option, or whose circumstances rule it out, usually find it necessary to give thought to the question of how they will spend time with their spiritual friends. In such cases, the process of developing and deepening spiritual friendships takes rather longer and requires a bit more conscious planning. The important thing is to ensure that one meets up with spiritual friends regularly and frequently in conditions that provide ample opportunity to relax and talk freely and fully. I think it is also important occasionally to get away from one's daily environment and spend longer blocks of time with one's spiritual friends – including retreats on which one can practise and discuss the Dharma with them.

Those who have parental responsibilities can find it challenging (especially when they also have demanding jobs) to fit in substantial periods of time with friends. However, I know of plenty of examples that prove it can be done. Here again, it may just be a question of accepting that the process may take a little longer. Obviously, things get easier if one can get some help with one's responsibilities. For Buddhist parents, it might be a good strategy to look for opportunities to cooperate with each other in groups – developing friendships with one another, and providing mutual assistance with child-care responsibilities, so as to help each other to get away on retreat, or to visit other spiritual friends. I hope that as the number of committed Buddhists in our society grows, such opportunities for mutual help will increase.

Duties of body, speech, and mind

I argued in Chapter 5 that when we enter a friendship, benevolence ripens into intimacy, and intimacy into personal obligation. Any kind of friendship thus brings with it a sense of duty, and this sense is likely to be especially strong when a friendship is 'in the good'.

But perhaps I need to make clear what the word 'duty' might mean in a Buddhist context. A duty is an intention that asserts its moral priority over other impulses that oppose or compete with it. A duty is perceived as such only when we feel some conflict between what we know we should do and some other desire.

Duties are usually thought of as things imposed on us from outside, whether by convention, law, or God. Consequently, the desire to do one's duty may sometimes be at bottom no more than the desire to avoid punishment or social disgrace. Clearly, the duties of friendship (and especially of spiritual friendship) aren't like that. Kalyāṇa mitratā is not laid on us like a burden, but springs from our authentic desire for the kalyāṇa. Nevertheless, the love of the kalyāṇa exists in us side by side with other desires, and they will often submerge our love of the kalyāṇa, if we don't constantly renew our choice – preferring the true-good-beautiful above the claims of comfort, pleasure, security, and so on. Staying in touch with our love of the kalyāṇa, and trying to live from it, is the most important part of what Buddhism means by 'mindfulness'.

The duties of friendship thus derive from our own hearts – from our inward sense of what is most true and important in life – and not from any external authority. We could therefore call them 'heartfelt duties'. A heartfelt duty rests not on the usual opposition between inward desire and outward obligation, but on the idea of a hierarchy of desires, in which śraddhā, the love of the kalyāṇa, is supreme.

What, then, are the heartfelt duties of friendship? They can be divided broadly into three kinds, corresponding to the three levels of action recognized in traditional Buddhist teaching. Of these, outward or bodily action is only the first. Our thoughts count as actions too – very subtle ones. But positioned between these two is a third level of action: speech. Our words impinge on the minds of others and so – to the extent that their actions are influenced by our speech – upon the physical world.

The next two chapters will be concerned respectively with the duties of spiritual friendship in speech and mind. To conclude the present chapter, I will consider the bodily or practical duties.

Bodily duties: practical help and generosity

Spiritual friendship emerges from the love of the kalyāṇa. In that sense it is distinct from ordinary friendship. But that doesn't mean that spiritual friends only share rarefied, 'spiritual' concerns, and ignore each other's practical needs. Far from it. To use an ancient metaphor, two spiritual friends should be like a pair of hands, one of which naturally and automatically assists the other in whatever task it happens to be doing.[84] The bodily duties of friendship are very simple. They boil down to practical help and generosity. Firstly, let's consider practical help.

About twelve years ago, I was running the office that handles administration for my order. At that time, the volume of work was growing rapidly, but I had no assistant. Eventually I was snowed under with paperwork. I had been struggling hard to keep on top of it, and felt exhausted and a bit demoralized. In this mood, I received a telephone call from a close friend, Devamitra. We talked about this and that, but he quickly noticed my low spirits, and made me explain what was bothering me. I then heard him saying, 'Well, I'll come up to help you for the next couple of weeks.' I was startled by the offer, because he had just been explaining his plans to do something else. I remember saying, 'No, no, Devamitra, it's important that you stick to your plans.' But he insisted, 'No, I would prefer to come and help you.'

Two days later, Devamitra arrived, and over the next fortnight he did all my filing, typed numerous letters, and generally made himself as useful as he could. If he felt any regret for his abandoned plans, he didn't show it. In fact, he seemed very happy to be with me, lending a hand. His cheerful presence helped me as much as his hard work.

Devamitra's sacrifice of two weeks from his busy schedule was a great kindness. Sometimes, small kindnesses can be equally moving. For three months during the summer of 1989 I co-led a retreat with another good friend of mine – Suvajra. Throughout those months I was very busy writing talks and planning activities, but at the same time I was still supposed to do my share of the practical chores. There were occasions when I would glance at the roster and realize I had absent-mindedly overlooked a duty, such as helping to cook, or washing up after a meal. I would then ask the others assigned to that task, 'What happened? Did you just manage without me?' 'Oh, no,' they replied, 'Suvajra did it for you.' Suvajra knew how busy I was: he had been watching out for me and silently stepping in to fill any gaps that might arise from my preoccupation.

I imagine my two examples speak for themselves, but a few details might be worth highlighting. Firstly, on seeing my difficulty, Devamitra and Suvajra acted promptly and without hesitation. It seems they instantly accepted my needs (and my duties) as their own. A swift and wholehearted identification of oneself with one's friends is part of the beauty of true friendship. Secondly, they acted in person, making the necessary sacrifice of time and energy themselves. There may sometimes be good reasons for asking somebody else to help a friend on your behalf (you may not have the necessary skill or knowledge, for example). All the same, speaking for myself at least, I know I feel uneasy if a friend of mine has a problem and I am doing nothing to help directly.

Thirdly, Devamitra and Suvajra did not wait for me to ask them for help. They just tuned in to my need, without any request – or even a hint – from me, and took the initiative. If you assume that your friends are OK because they are not actually complaining, you may end up doing very little for them. Perhaps they will never ask, because they are so anxious to avoid bothering you, even when they are in terrible difficulties. In making the same point, al-Ghazālī said, 'To oblige [a brother] to ask is the ultimate shortcoming in brotherly duty.'[85] That is a challenging statement, because while your friends' needs may sometimes be obvious (when they are ill, for example), they may at other times be outwardly invisible. The only way you can intuit their needs is by knowing your friends deeply, and making the effort to find out what is going on in their lives right now.

The fourth and final point I want to highlight is that neither Devamitra nor Suvajra expected anything in return for their kind actions. Mettā has no interest in balancing the books. The thought that a friend 'owes me a favour' may be a natural enough attitude in friendships based on use, but it doesn't belong in those that are based on the kalyāṇa.

I know of a Buddhist in India – let's call him Vidya – who, while quite poor, comes from a higher caste than most of his Buddhist friends. At one time, Vidya's daughter fell dangerously ill and needed an operation. Unfortunately, Vidya didn't have the money to pay for it. He turned to his relatives for help, but for some reason they couldn't or wouldn't give any. But on hearing of Vidya's problem, his Buddhist friends, all poor themselves, quickly said, 'Don't worry. Just go ahead and arrange the operation. We'll get the cash, and help you to pay it back later.' They then rooted around for the money, somehow finding part of it themselves, and standing as guarantors for loans to cover the rest. They also arranged for blood donors. (In India, it seems, if you draw on a blood bank for an operation, you have to arrange to replenish it by an equivalent amount.) Vidya hadn't expected or looked for this kind of practical assistance from his spiritual friends. And although he already knew in principle that the sangha should transcend caste, it invigorated his faith to see that his spiritual friends were ready – even though they came from a lower caste than his own – to help him in what he had at first regarded as a family matter.

The action of Vidya's friends perfectly exemplified 'showing concern for [one's friends'] children', which the *Sigālaka Sutta* lists as one of the practical duties of friendship. I think this duty actually has an even more fundamental and general form. The point is that, when we feel strongly for friends, we don't just care about them individually: we also care for those whom *they* care for.

I would add that we also care for *what* they care for, particularly when their care springs from their love of the kalyāṇa. On this topic, the example that comes to my mind concerns two people I used to know in the early years of my involvement with Buddhism. In telling the story here, I'll call them Geoff and

Martin. Geoff had dreams of raising the profile of Buddhism in religious education in Britain. He made a start by teaching a regular evening course on Buddhism at a local adult education institute. The course was certainly unusual and perhaps unique in those far-off days, but due to Geoff's enthusiasm and skill it became popular. At this point, sadly, Geoff died before being able to take his dreams any further.

After getting over his friend's death, one of the questions facing Martin was what to do about the course. He didn't want the responsibility himself – he had his own projects to attend to. But he was keenly aware of what the course had meant to his friend: aware of Geoff's passionate enthusiasm for the project, of his achievement in persuading the college to mount the course, of all the work Geoff had put into making a success of it, and of the hopes he'd had for its future. At that time, there were very few people around who could teach Buddhism at all – and certainly not with the enthusiasm and first-hand knowledge that Geoff had brought to it. But now he was dead. Was the course going to die too? Martin couldn't see any alternative but to take on the task himself. The last I heard, Martin was still teaching the course, some years later. Perhaps he had come to enjoy it, but his original motivation was not his own wishes but his feeling for Geoff.

The second bodily duty of friendship is generosity or giving. Of course, this isn't really a different duty from practical help: they often amount to the same thing. Generosity is the same principle of helpfulness, as applied to possessions.

The importance of giving is stressed in all forms of Buddhism, and in the Mahāyāna tradition it is the first of six (or ten) 'perfections', transcendental virtues to be developed by bodhisattvas (those who aspire to become Buddhas). In principle, all living beings are the object of the bodhisattva's generosity, but in practice, as finite creatures, we have to make some practical decisions about who to focus on. The tradition makes it clear that our practice of giving should start with those who are nearby: our family, if we have one, and our friends. If we aren't generous to the people who are part of our daily life, our generosity to others may be no more than a sentimental compensation for a refusal to transform our actual relationships. Friends should be prominent among the objects of our generosity, not just because they are near at hand but also because we have first-hand knowledge of their needs: in their case, we are well positioned to give appropriate help, and can get immediate feedback on its effects.

I commonly observe many acts of material generosity in the spiritual community to which I belong. For example, if somebody lacks the funds for some purpose – to go on a retreat, for example, or for some special medical treatment – an appeal usually produces the necessary cash in a pretty short time. Indeed, as the levels of mutual trust and goodwill are so high, such generosity probably flows almost as much between those who know each other only slightly, or not at all, as it does between close friends.

However, one distinctive form that generosity can take in the context of friendship is the tendency to share possessions. In the case of spiritual friends who live together, this sharing sometimes amounts to common ownership of what is nominally personal property. I myself experience this tendency in the house in which I live with Buddhist friends. I am happy for any other member of the household to come into my room in my absence and take something of mine, and I know the others reciprocate that trust. We all know that each individual in the house will take only what he needs, and will consider others' needs before his own. Naturally, sharing comes more easily to people who are living a relatively simple life and not accumulating material possessions. After all, the more you own, the more anxious you tend to be about holding on to it.

Generosity encompasses more than material things. There is generosity with time, for example. In our modern culture of ruthless efficiency, we may be rather weak in this department, at least by comparison with cultures that have not travelled so far from their traditional roots.

A friend of mine once told me a story that illustrates the point. While teaching English in South-East Asia, he used to give an advanced class to a small group of mature students. All four students in the group were under great pressure of work: each of them held major managerial responsibilities while also struggling to carry out part-time doctoral degree programmes in the foreign medium of English.

My teacher friend and his four students got on very well together, and they all soon came to regard one another as friends. One afternoon, he asked them if they would mind finishing the class a little early, to give him time to get through the congested urban streets to attend an interview for a job at a university. 'Oh,' they said, 'you're going for an interview? Yes, of course: we'll finish early – and we'll all go with you! We'll wait, and root for you while you are being interviewed.' And so they did – one of the students using his car to ferry the whole group to the university through the heavy late-afternoon traffic. After the interview, the students took the teacher to a restaurant to treat him to dinner and talk about how the interview had gone. At the end of the evening, they drove him back to his apartment before making their own way home.

My friend couldn't help but feel touched to see such busy people giving up several hours, purely on impulse, for the sake of friendship. In the West, most of us simply wouldn't think it a rational use of our time to tag along with a friend just to give him moral support at a job interview. Nevertheless, my teacher friend noticed that, by such gestures as these, the students created a very positive atmosphere that nourished his friendships with them – which, apparently, have continued at long distance since his return to the UK.

In addition to being the first of the perfections, giving shows up again further down the list – and here its relevance to spiritual friendship becomes even more explicit. It is part of the seventh perfection (in the list of ten), which is known as skilful means (*upāya kauśalya*). This perfection is, in essence, the bodhisattva's ability to reach out to living beings and communicate with them on their own terms, for a bodhisattva must arouse and nurture their faith in the Three Jewels in ways that appeal to them as they actually are, rather than in a spirit of 'Here it is: take it or leave it!'

In the context of skilful means, generosity appears as the first of a set of four qualities (known as the four *saṃgrahavastus*) that bring people together – and then keep them together – in a sangha or spiritual community. (The other three qualities, by the way, are loving speech, beneficial activity, and exemplification of the teaching.) The scholar Robert Thurman translates *saṃgrahavastu* as 'means of unification' and he defines this set of four qualities as 'the four ways in which a bodhisattva forms a group of people united by the common aim of practising the Dharma'.[86]

In other words, while we should certainly practise it as widely as possible, generosity does have a special function in building the spiritual community. Together with the other three 'means of unification' it creates within the sangha a mood of mutual gratitude, trust, and affection that makes the sangha strong and attracts new people to it. In a thriving spiritual community, the members are always giving to each other in one way or another – giving material things, but also giving practical assistance, and giving time and energy. Their mutual feelings of mettā and śraddhā find expression in this interchange of gifts, and that interchange reinforces the feelings that gave it birth. In such an atmosphere of friendliness, individual friendships can proliferate, put down deep roots, and bear abundant spiritual fruit.

10

Brahma and a Nightingale

The Duties of Speech in Friendship

A sensitive concern for speech is one of the hallmarks of Buddhist ethics. The words we hear – and those we speak – often have loud and long reverberations on our mental states. Buddhism understands speech as a 'door' of action, poised between the mental and physical realms – a kind of channel through which the human mind acts on the world for good or ill. What we say may bring karmic consequences just as weighty as those following what we *do*.

When the Buddhist scriptures refer to speech, they usually mention four kinds to be avoided – falsehood, slander, harshness, and idle chatter. Conversely, four opposite kinds of speech are to be cultivated: the ideal Buddhist is truthful, creates only harmony and not discord between others, speaks gently and pleasingly, and says only such things as are worthy to be heard.

These four principles mark the boundaries of skilful communication in any situation. In this chapter my aim is not to explore them in general, but to see how they apply to communication between spiritual friends. In that context, we can interpret the four principles in terms of speech that is truthful, faithful, loving, and helpful. I will say something about each of these qualities, leaving faithful speech till last as it belongs in a category distinct from the others. (It deals with how to speak *about* friends, rather than *to* them.)

Truthfulness

> *Having abandoned false speech, [a bhikkhu] abstains from falsehood. He speaks only the truth, he lives devoted to the truth; trustworthy and reliable, he does not deceive anyone in the world.*[87]

Truthfulness is obviously necessary for friendship. You may not feel angry when you discover a friend has lied to you – it depends on the exact nature of the case. However, you will probably wonder how well you know him or her, and whether there really is a friendship between you.

But in friendship, truthfulness involves much more than not telling lies. There must also be psychological truthfulness, or (as the *Sigālaka Sutta* puts it) the sharing of secrets. That calls for honesty about the deeper or hidden aspects of ourselves, the things that make us feel vulnerable or embarrassed. In ordinary friendships, this opening up is often very selective and partial, but in our closer spiritual friendships it needs to be wholehearted.

Perhaps a word of caution might be useful here. I am not suggesting that we relate to our spiritual friends as if they were our psychotherapists. There have been occasions when a new acquaintance, seeing me as a sort of Buddhist counsellor, has treated me to an exhaustive account of his childhood traumas as soon as we took our first stroll around the park together. I didn't mind, but it wasn't really a step towards friendship. Openness in spiritual friendship is not a clinical regime – just the cultivation of a natural tendency.

A more serious danger of this rather artificial kind of candour is that it will be abused. A naive belief in total psychological and moral transparency is wide open to manipulation. Within a spiritual group that subscribes to this kind of openness, individuals are vulnerable to exploitation by charismatic leaders. Such a leader may coax or bully weak and inexperienced disciples to 'open up' to him or her, with the aim of making them more dependent on his or her approval. When somebody you regard as a spiritual friend starts to *demand* openness from you as a right, you can be sure that something has gone wrong.

In practice, the value of openness always depends on the context. Even in genuine spiritual groups (not just in cults), some individuals may exploit self-disclosure, perhaps unconsciously, as a mask for selfish ends: they may, for example, invoke 'honesty about my feelings' as a pretext for making a sexual advance, or they may appeal to 'sincerity' as an excuse for saying something hurtful to someone they dislike. In the age of pop psychology and universal informality, openness can easily become a convenient slogan for rationalizing unethical impulses.

None of this in any way reduces the value and importance of openness. Psychological truthfulness *is* necessary in spiritual friendship, but it is also something of an art. To practise it effectively, we have to know what it is we really need to say, how to put it, and the right moment to speak. These skills are learned gradually, through experience, aided by the self-knowledge gained in meditation and the example set by more experienced friends.

In addition to psychological truthfulness, spiritual friendship also requires ethical truthfulness. Śraddhā, the heart's response to the kalyāṇa, inevitably shines a moral light inwards upon one's mental life and the secrets of one's past. When we are troubled by the awareness of having done something out of tune with the kalyāṇa, or indulged in unwholesome mental states, the natural response is to disclose it to our spiritual friends.

Confession is a traditional Buddhist practice. The Buddha welcomed confessions, as, for example, in his words to King Ajātasattu:

> *Since you have seen your transgression as a transgression and make amends for it according to the Dhamma, we acknowledge it. For, great king, this is growth in the discipline of the Noble One: that a person sees his transgression as a transgression, makes amends for it according to the Dhamma, and achieves restraint in the future.*[88]

To understand its importance, we have to see confession in the context of the spiritual life as a whole. The simplest classification of the Buddhist path is in terms of morality, meditation, and wisdom. Although we have to work on all three from the start, we won't get very far with meditation and wisdom until we have put morality on a very strong footing. Confession is the key to success in that task.

Actually, the word for 'morality' (*śīla*) literally means 'behaviour': it refers to whatever we do, say, or think in day to day life, as seen from the viewpoint of the Dharma. But seeing ourselves from that perspective isn't easy. At first, we may not be very clearly aware of the way we behave (especially our patterns of speech and thought), or how well it accords with our spiritual ideal. Many of us don't clearly see our own faults, or if we do, we may indulge them because we think them too trivial to bother about. Often, too, we act or talk in ways that, while not really 'bad', nevertheless squander our energy or just coarsen our consciousness. Insensitive to such subtle dimensions of *śīla*, we may take it for granted that our behaviour is 'good enough'. Sooner or later, we find ourselves wondering why we find it so hard to progress in meditation. Meghiya, whom we met in Chapter 1, is a good example.

Progress in meditation depends as much on what we do when we are *not* meditating as it does on any particular technique we use while actually sitting on the cushion. I notice that many sincere Buddhists, despite their ideals, live rather distracted lives outside the confines of their meditation practice. We have to look for progress and refinement in *śīla* before we can hope for much in our meditation. Experience has taught me that the best way to do this is through the regular practice of confession. And the proper context for confession – perhaps the only framework in which it can be practised fully – is spiritual friendship.

As unenlightened beings, we are held earthbound by the unwholesome roots of greed, hatred, and delusion, together with all their ramifying rootlets: petty selfishness, minor resentments, self-flattering views, and so on. The more that genuine spiritual inspiration arises, the more it will bring not only joy but also a healthy sense of shame. Shame, in the Buddhist sense, is not irrational guilt or self-loathing, but more like the frustration that arises from balked enthusiasm, the felt tension between śraddhā and the impulses that oppose it.

To put it another way, it is as if a web of sticky, tensile threads is constantly pulling us back from our spiritual journey. The threads are really part of us – our own negative tendencies. Shame is the uncomfortable sense of a filament entangling an arm or leg. We can't press ahead until we pay attention to that sensation, and break the thread. We can then move on a bit further, until we feel another thread growing tight. Spiritual life is thus a constant disentangling-to-move-on. We start by loosening the tightest strands, but as we go forward we become sensitive to gossamer threads that we didn't notice when we began.

When first taking up confession, some people bring to it feelings of self-dislike left over from their previous religious or family conditioning. But confession should spring from śraddhā, not guilt. It produces a joyful inner lightness that the scriptures call 'delight'.[89] This state is the necessary psychological basis for the relaxed concentration of meditative states. Understanding it in this way, and learning from the example of more mature friends, one can learn how to distinguish healthy shame from irrational guilt, and so confess effectively.

The limitation of my simile of the web is that it pictures an individual trying to break out in isolation. Actually, few of us would ever muster enough energy or sense of direction to get free on our own. This brings us back to a point I made in Chapter 1, when discussing the *Meghiya Sutta*. There are two forms of healthy shame: the kind that springs from one's own ethical sense, and 'shame through respect for the wise' (*apatrāpya*). What this means is that, in the early phases of spiritual life, one's private conscience is too crude to guide one out of the web. One needs spiritual friends, especially more mature ones, whose example can fine-tune one's ethical feelings. This doesn't mean blindly accepting your friends' moral judgements as superior to your own: *apatrāpya* is a glad appreciation of the kalyāṇa in others, not a dependence on perceived authority.

As well as stimulating *apatrāpya*, spiritual friends satisfy our need for someone who can actually *hear* our confessions. In Chapter 7, I suggested that we only fully become ourselves through communication with friends. Confession is the ethical dimension of this general truth. An inward, silent acknowledgement of a fault is vital, but we gain a greater spiritual benefit if we also communicate that inward acknowledgement to someone who can understand and appreciate it. Through communication, the nature of the fault and one's rejection of it somehow become clearer and more decisive, while things that stay unspoken tend to remain cloudy and tentative. Spiritual friends are essential here. Other sorts of friends don't share the commitment to the kalyāṇa that makes confession meaningful, and they may just be embarrassed if we try to confess to them.

In the order I belong to, we practise confession in a variety of ways. It often happens spontaneously (and sometimes as a regular practice) between pairs of order members who are close friends. It is also practised more systematically in the regular meetings of chapters – small local groups of the order. It is perhaps the most important way (though by no means the only one) in which the members of a chapter communicate with one another as spiritual friends.

I myself practise confession in both these ways. My old friend Sona and I usually spend some time together every day when we are both at home, and our conversation often includes a confessional element. Then, in my weekly chapter meeting, I go more deeply into the main themes emerging from this daily process. The chapter is an ethical and spiritual mirror in which I can see ever more clearly the image of my going for refuge. The other members of a chapter play an important part in clarifying that image – a point I will come back to later, in discussing the principle of helpful speech.

Loving speech

Having abandoned harsh speech, he refrains from harsh speech. He speaks only such words as are gentle, pleasing to the ear, endearing, going to the heart, polite, amiable and agreeable to the manyfolk.[90]

The second of the four great principles of ethical speech is that speech should be gentle and pleasing. This really means that it should be based on love – imbued with mettā.

But mettā depends on awareness. Communication between friends flows from an awareness that is deeper and more specific than is possible between strangers. Conversely, the effort to cultivate awareness will deepen friendship. Kindly speaking is therefore inseparable from kindly listening and kindly watching. It requires sensitive attention to what one's friend is doing and saying. This attentiveness gradually leads to the power to intuit his or her feelings and thoughts.

Perhaps the first thing to be aware of at any time is whether a friend actually *wants* to communicate. Loving speech includes knowing when to be silent, and this involves learning to recognize one's friends' mood signals. One also needs to know their sore spots, the topics that are painful for them. You should not force on them a subject when they show signs of not wanting to go into it, or pry into matters they are not yet ready to share. This sort of tactful sensitivity is very different from mere shyness or indifference, and you may need to learn to distinguish which you are really showing.

When the time does come to speak, the next duty of loving speech is to refrain from harshness. Harsh speech can be of two kinds: direct and indirect. Direct harsh speech springs from feelings of resentment, anger, or cruelty. Nothing is so destructive of friendship as direct harsh speech. Indeed, it can be the death not of one friendship alone but of a whole spiritual community, if a dispute flares up within it, leading to faction and schism. A vital precept, then, between friends and throughout the spiritual community as a whole, is *not to take offence*. Effective observance of the precept depends on mindfulness of one's mental states. You have to learn to recognize not just your friend's sore spots, but also your own.

Sometimes, even a neutral intellectual discussion can suddenly become polarized. Discussion of the Dharma is one of the great blessings of spiritual friendship, but one needs to engage in it sensitively, especially with a friend one is still getting to know. If you are a 'wisdom type' (the kind of person who is full of intellectual enthusiasm for the Dharma) you may be eager to demonstrate your understanding, and that might make you rather quick and forceful in challenging 'wrong views'. But for some people – and your friend may be one of them – an unmolested confusion may be a necessary stage in the journey towards independent clarity. The best way to help such people clarify their ideas is by listening to them, and helping them draw out their thoughts, without pushing your own angle.

There are subtle forms of direct harsh speech. In this connection, it can be spiritually useful to take an honest look at one's use of humour. Play and humour are part of being human. They even seem to be part of *enlightened* humanity: a delightful vein of gentle irony lends charm to some of the Buddha's suttas. A good example is the tale of a monk with psychic powers who ascends to heaven in order to pose Brahmā (God) a knotty cosmological question. Unable to sidetrack the monk with blustering and evasive answers, the deity finally has to take him aside, out of earshot of the angels, to admit that he doesn't know the answer. He scolds the monk for inappropriately coming to him with profound questions, when the best person to solve such riddles – as the monk really should have known – is the Buddha.[91]

Playfulness, far from being taboo, can be part of skilful speech. But – let's face it – it can sometimes be unskilful. Most of us, at some time or other, have wrapped up a half-conscious desire to wound inside a joke. Strangely, we are most likely to do this with friends, with whom we feel little polite caution. Even when such teasing is actually innocent, with no harm meant, its effect can be more hurtful than we realize (or than our friends let show).

Unlike direct harsh speech, the indirect variety does not flow from antagonism. It may just be a way of letting off steam. We all sometimes allow our talk to be tainted with emotional sourness of one sort or another, if only mildly and intermittently. A common example is cynicism – the habit of dwelling on the bad side of the human race (or, more often, some particular section of it). There are lots of people, including some Buddhists, who seem surprisingly interested in talking about the faults of one category of people or another. Within a spiritual community, cynicism may take the form of finding fault in aspects of the community's culture and institutions. Of course, such things should be open to constructive critical discussion, but one needs to avoid falling into a habit of carping. Sometimes, when shared with others, this kind of cynicism may become the basis of a friendship, which then becomes an alliance of 'outs'. But animosity is a bad foundation for spiritual friendship, which should be *for* the kalyāṇa, not against anything or anyone.

Indirect harshness can also include unthinkingly giving vent to pessimistic moods. 'Sounding off' is different from genuine self-disclosure. Then there are the various kinds of *crude* speech: coarseness is a facile way of releasing tension and creating the wrong kind of intimacy based on a superficial idea of 'being natural'.

We should also be very careful about how, if at all, we pass on to our friends negative things we have heard other people say about them. In most cases, the best option is to keep it from them, otherwise one becomes a postman, delivering hate mail to one's friends. In mentioning such things, one not only hurts them, but probably also causes an ethically negative state of resentment to arise in their minds. When you hear someone say bad things about your friend, the best way to deal with it is to counter it actively yourself. This point, however, really belongs to the section on faithful speech, below.

Loving speech calls for much more than abstinence from harshness, just as gardening requires more than pulling up weeds. Its positive side consists in giving voice to mettā. In the Buddhist tradition, an important way of doing this is the practice of rejoicing in merits. We saw in Chapter 2 how gladly and spontaneously the Buddha's two great disciples, Sāriputta and Moggallāna, expressed appreciation of each other's qualities. Friends have a livelier appreciation of one another's merits than other people can, and should celebrate those merits freely. When this habit is established in a spiritual community, it creates a confident, joyful atmosphere that strengthens that community and attracts others towards it, helping the sangha to grow. The principle of truthful speech ensures that such rejoicing is not just well-meant flattery.

We should be pleased, too, when we hear other people speaking well of our friends, and should pass on to them any good things we've heard said about them. And when you are the recipient of the rejoicing, there is also a kind of duty of graceful acceptance: if a friend sincerely praises you, in private or in public, allow yourself to feel pleased (without getting intoxicated) and to show your pleasure. Why fussily qualify compliments, or coolly shrug off praise? (This point is especially for the benefit of those conditioned by dour, self-effacing Protestant cultures!)

Then there is the expression of sympathy. Mettā is an emotion that leads towards the exchange of self and other: through mettā, your friends' happiness and pain become your own. Part of the duty of loving speech is to show them as much. In Buddhist scriptures, mettā is closely associated with *anukampā*, a word that literally means 'vibrating with'. This vibration has two pitches: sympathetic joy (*muditā*) and the compassionate participation in sorrow (*karuṇā*). Like mettā, these are universal emotions, not to be exclusively reserved for one's friends. But just as mettā finds its natural perfection in friendship, so sympathetic joy and compassion ripen into personal duties in friendship: we share in our friends' triumphs and troubles in a direct, personal way. This implies taking some interest in what they are interested in (so giving them opportunities to express their enthusiasms), and likewise showing concern for their sorrow: drawing out its causes, and helping them to remedy or come to terms with it.

The positive counterpart of avoiding coarseness is the effort to refine one's speech. Communication that arises from love of the kalyāṇa naturally tends towards the beautiful, not in meaning alone, but even in form. In speaking to friends, mettā should make us mindful of our choice of words and tone. Mañjuśrī, the bodhisattva of wisdom, is also sometimes called Mañjughoṣa, 'the gentle-voiced one'. The Buddha himself, according to tradition, had cultivated loving speech in many former lives. As a result, his voice was compared to that of Brahma, and to the song of the *karavīka*, the Indian nightingale. In other words, his voice had the resonance of a god's utterance, combined with a sweetly musical quality.[92]

Helpful speech

> *Having abandoned idle chatter, he abstains from idle chatter. He speaks at the right time, speaks what is factual and beneficial, speaks on the Dhamma and the Discipline. His words are worth treasuring; they are timely, backed by reasons, measured, and connected with the good.*[93]

The third principle is that speech should be useful, or helpful. When you have been practising meditation intensively for a while – let's say when you have just returned from a retreat – it can be rather jarring to take part in conventional social gatherings. In such a situation, you may start to see just why the Dharma values silence so highly. To begin with, you might notice how rapid and continuous the talk is, then how randomly it hops from one subject to another, and perhaps how insignificant, in the last analysis, much of the content is. Afterwards, you may find yourself oddly drained of energy, your mind somehow tarnished.

The Buddha considered idle chatter so antagonistic to spiritual practice that he made it the subject of a separate speech precept. It comes as rather a jolt to realize that, in a sense, this puts it on a par with the obvious evils of untruthfulness, harsh speech, and slander. Unfortunately, the context where we are most likely to overindulge in trivial speech is with friends, so we need to make a special effort to reduce it in the context of spiritual friendship.

The practice of silence can be very valuable here. Anuruddha, Nandiya, and Kimbila maintained silence – in the context of full and loving mutual awareness – for five days at a time. Then they passed the fifth night in talk of the Dharma. Except when we are on retreat, we are unlikely to find that a feasible lifestyle, but we can try to express the principle behind it in a way appropriate to our own situation; that is, we can make an effort to reduce meaningless speech, and to make sure that our daily life includes periods of silence.

We customarily associate silence with solitude but, strange as it may seem, it is also part of friendship. Silences are not necessarily gaps in communication. When friends are with one another, the absence of words need not divide them. In fact, it may sometimes unite them in a deeper mutual awareness than they find when talking. In the weekly meetings of my order chapter, we try to allow all our speech to emerge out of – and merge back into – silence. Sometimes a silence continues for a long time, and we don't seem to feel an anxious need to fill it with something.

I am not trying to mystify silence: it is not a force in its own right, but simply a valuable means of creating a space in which awareness can dwell on what is most essential – mutual śraddhā and mettā.

When they did speak, Anuruddha and his friends discussed the Dharma. Most of us would find speaking of nothing but the Dharma a dry affair, if we understood the Dharma as including only 'Buddhism' in the strict sense. However, the Buddha himself didn't interpret it so narrowly, so presumably we don't have to. He explained that 'the Dharma and the Discipline' included not just his own words, but whatever helped the individual to develop spiritually in accordance with certain defining principles.[94]

Taking this broadly (as I think we should) we can include in our conception of the Dharma, in addition to the core of traditional Buddhist doctrines and practices, many other things that refine the mind, or illuminate the understanding. To give a

personal example, I take whatever chances I get to see perform-
ances of Shakespeare, and I love to talk about them with friends
who share my interest. I don't consider that an indulgence in idle
chatter. Such interests can function as both branches and roots of
our spiritual life: they simultaneously express and nourish the
heart's response to the kalyāṇa. Of course, we need to keep a wise
balance between the growth of the branches and the strength of
the trunk. Other interests cease to be spiritually beneficial when
they preoccupy us so much that we neglect Buddhist practice in
the primary sense. And we defeat our spiritual purpose when we
over-stimulate the discursive mind by indulging in too much talk
(even talk about Buddhism).

According to the dictionary definition, a kalyāṇa mitra is a
'virtuous friend'. One variety of helpful speech is therefore
speech that enhances a friend's virtue. Only Buddhas are ethically perfect, so until they have become Buddhas even virtuous
friends are bound to have faults. Helping each other to overcome
such weaknesses is part of the shared enterprise of spiritual
friendship.

There will inevitably be occasions when we see close
friends doing things that don't fit with the ideals that we share
with them – lying, perhaps, or smoking a joint, or backbiting
about a mutual acquaintance – and seeming not to notice any contradiction. While we need to choose our moment carefully, it
doesn't make sense to turn a blind eye to such things indefinitely.
Unfortunately, the word 'admonition', the technical term for this
aspect of helpful speech, smacks of frowning and finger wagging,
and these have no place in friendship. The point is that friendship
means developing enough mutual trust and mettā to be able to
question one another's behaviour. The principle of kindly speech
should ensure that this is done with tact and warmth, and at a
well-chosen moment.

There are two aspects to this mutual questioning. The first
concerns your friends' faults in relation to yourself: thoughtless

things they have said or done that hurt you. The other concerns their unskilful actions towards other people.

As regards the first category, I recommend that, as far as possible, you simply try to be patient and forgive your friends when they tread on your toes. If you are too quick to admonish friends for things that irritate you personally, it might mean that you are less interested in loving them than in showing them how to love *you*. But, as we have seen, the essence of friendship consists in loving rather than being loved. Admittedly, one has to take account of one's limits. You may find that, despite your attempts to be patient, a friend's behaviour is so upsetting that it threatens the future of the friendship, and in that situation you can hardly avoid broaching the subject.

The second category – your friend's behaviour towards other people – is different. If you see a friend doing things that wrong others, the question is not how long you yourself can put up with it. One then has a duty to put some questions to the friend, and to lose no time in doing so.

Undeniably, this mutual moral challenge is a difficult part of helpful speech. Like the principle of psychological truthfulness, it can be abused: charismatic individuals can use moral language for selfish ends, manipulating the naive with false praise or blame. Admonition can also be a vehicle for unacknowledged personal animosity. But in our easy-going, non-judgemental culture, there is probably more danger that we will neglect this duty than overdo it. The acid test of one's ability to question a friend appropriately lies in one's willingness to be questioned oneself. If you can honestly welcome your friends' insights into your own behaviour, you can probably trust yourself to question *their* actions kindly and helpfully, without irritability or manipulative intent.

The key to success in mutual questioning is to make it a systematic part of one's spiritual life. This brings us back to the practice of confession. Regular confession among spiritual friends dissolves unease, as each friend becomes used to opening up, and to helping the others to purify their deeds, words, and thoughts. I have found that a small group of friends is ideal as a confessional setting. Ideally, such a group should be small enough to feel intimate, but big enough to produce a variety of perspectives. Although everyone in the group may be at the same level of spiritual maturity, its shared strengths can allow it to function like a more mature friend to each individual member. This is what I described earlier as 'the exchange of the kalyāṇa'.

Such a group of friends helps each member to confess. It does this mainly by just listening to his or her confessions with sympathetic understanding. Sometimes this listening may be enough. Sometimes, though, after hearing you confess, your friends' thoughtful listening may lead them to ask you questions, or make comments. They may point out some way in which you should make amends for any harm you have caused other people. Their words can often lead you to a deeper understanding of the state of mind that made you do whatever you have confessed, and so help you to avoid such moods in future.

Faithful speech

> *Having abandoned slander, he abstains from slander. He does not repeat elsewhere what he has heard here in order to divide others from the people here, nor does he repeat here what he has heard elsewhere in order to divide these from the people there. Thus he is a reconciler of those who are divided and a promoter of friendships. Rejoicing, delighting, and exulting in concord, he speaks only words that are conducive to concord.*[95]

With the fourth principle, we move from the private to the public aspect of speech. The wider significance of this principle is to avoid slander and backbiting, and conversely to foster harmony between other people. In the context of friendship, the specific application of the principle is to speak to others in a way that is faithful to our friends, whether or not they are present when we speak.

For example, just as truthful speech includes revealing our own secrets, so faithful speech includes strictly keeping those of our friends. We should know intuitively when something confided in the intimacy of friendship is not to be mentioned to others, even if the friend has not explicitly said so.

The ability to keep secrets is a good test of character and will. The attention and interest that one gets from other people by disclosing to them some juicy bit of information about a mutual acquaintance is always tempting. Relaxed chit-chat in small groups, or with a lover, is the kind of setting in which one may let slip things about friends that one should really keep hidden. How to overcome that weakness? I think it can be a useful exercise to practise keeping something – almost anything – secret: resolving not to disclose some fascinating morsel of news or information, even when you are morally free to do so. (Obviously, you shouldn't conceal things that others need to know!) If you develop this capacity, you will be more able to guard a friend's privacy when the need arises.

Keeping secrets is part of a wider duty to protect and foster your friends' reputation (in accordance with truthfulness, of course). As their second self, you should guard their good name as carefully as your own. In fact, more so: the Dharma teaches us to cultivate indifference to the 'worldly winds' of praise or blame, and of fame or notoriety; but it is a betrayal of friendship to air the faults of friends behind their backs. Likewise, to permit someone else to attack one's friends' good name would be like idly standing by while someone burgles their house.

Generally, then, however keenly one feels a friend's faults, it is not appropriate to talk about those faults to other people. When we hear such faults mentioned by others, we can always make a tactful attempt to redirect the conversation, or to redress the balance by correcting any inaccuracy, or by speaking in the friend's praise. In general, one should aim to be loyal to friends in such situations, without indignantly taking offence on their behalf.

Obviously, it is all right to discuss a friend's weaknesses in a confessional group, where the friend is present and has offered or agreed to discuss the matter. There are also times when you might have to discuss friends' failings in their absence, for their own good, with other members of the spiritual community. When someone gets into personal difficulties, for instance, some discussion of his or her mistakes or bad habits may be an unpalatable but necessary part of helping to sort out the problem.

But setting aside these special cases, it doesn't accord with the spirit of friendship to pick over a friend's faults with other people, like connoisseurs appraising an amateur painting. There are two challenges in such situations: to resist the mood of a group, and to shun the unwholesome pleasure of accurately skewering someone else's defects.

I have been speaking so far of faithful speech in situations where the friend is absent. But subtle kinds of disloyalty are also possible in his or her presence. One of these is the attempt to parade the friendship before others for the gratification of one's ego, by a self-regarding display of familiarity or affection. Teasing friends in public sometimes springs from similar motives.

In the Pali suttas, perhaps the most touching example of faithful speech between two friends is the Buddha's praise of Ānanda in the *Mahāparinibbāna Sutta*. Although sick and aware that his end was very near, the Buddha showed no concern for himself, but he did take thought for the effect his death would have on his lifelong friend. In the presence of the assembled monks, he summoned Ānanda in order to rejoice publicly in his merits. With perfect delicacy, he chose to do so by reassuring Ānanda that his long service as a personal attendant had been well performed, and marked with the dignity of a timeless pattern:

> *Then the Lord addressed the monks: 'Monks, all those who were Arahant fully-enlightened Buddhas in the past have had just such a chief attendant as Ānanda, and so too will those Blessed Lords who come in the future. Monks, Ānanda is wise. He knows when it is the right time for monks to come to see the Tathāgata, when it is the right time for nuns, for male lay-followers, for female lay-followers, for kings, for royal ministers, for leaders of other schools, and for their pupils.*
>
> *Ānanda has four remarkable and wonderful qualities. What are they? If a company of monks comes to see Ānanda, they are pleased at the sight of him, and when Ānanda talks Dhamma to them they are pleased, and when he is silent they are disappointed. And so it is, too, with nuns, with male and female lay-followers. And these four qualities apply to a wheel-turning monarch: if he is visited by a company of Khattiyas, of Brahmins, of householders, or of ascetics, they are pleased at the sight of him and when he talks to them, and when he is silent they are disappointed. And so too it is with Ānanda.'*[96]

11
The Mind's Eye

The Inner Dimension of Friendship

Finally, we come to the mental duties of friendship – which are perhaps the most essential, for Buddhism teaches that outward actions in word and deed all flow from states of mind.

First, we need to understand what is meant by 'mind'. In the Buddhist conception, it involves much more than the thinking function. The word *citta*, although often translated as 'mind', really unites the two faculties that in English we call 'mind' and 'heart': it includes the emotions and the will, not just cognition.

In essence, there is only one mental duty of spiritual friendship: to nurture the mettā and śraddhā that we feel for our friends. In this chapter, I am going to explore four aspects of this duty: mindfulness, trust, forgiveness, and fidelity.

Mindfulness: cultivating friendship in the heart

Everyone has some sense of moral obligation to friends, but few think in terms of actually nurturing their feelings of friendship.

Until we take up the spiritual life – and so start to evaluate our inner condition – we tend to identify with our existing emotions: for the most part, it doesn't occur to us to question or change them. We either like someone or we don't; and when we lose interest in somebody we used to like, we usually make little effort to reverse the cooling of our affection.

But if friendship is the whole of the spiritual life, we can't afford to be so passive. Instead, we ought to protect and develop mettā and śraddhā for our spiritual friends, recognizing that, if we fail to do so, those friendships will eventually fade, being dependent on conditions, as all things are. Our main tools for this task are the central methods of Buddhist practice: meditation and mindfulness.

The whole spiritual life can be understood as *bhāvanā*: the persistent cultivation of a range of positive emotions and thoughts. The *mettā bhāvanā*, for example, is 'the cultivation of friendliness'. Of the hundreds of meditation practices that have come down to us in the Buddhist tradition, this is one of the most valuable for today, offering us a healthy antidote to the effects of our individualistic and socially atomized culture. It involves the development of goodwill and is often divided into five stages. You start with yourself, and then go on to a good friend. Next, you call to mind someone you normally feel indifferent to, and extend the mettā to that person (mentally 'making friends' with him or her). The fourth step is to enlarge your friendliness still further to include someone that you dislike. In the fifth and final stage, you extend the feeling of mettā to encompass all living beings.

As this description shows, the main goal of the practice is a universal loving attitude: its aim is to develop friendliness in general rather than particular friendships. Nevertheless, it has the effect of strengthening one's existing friendships and fostering new ones.

Even so, I've often thought it would be useful to have, in addition to the mettā bhāvanā, a practice designed to cultivate particular friendships. The *guru yoga* of Tibetan Buddhism does this for one kind of friendship, but I am thinking here of something less vertical. Such a practice seems to have existed in the early Buddhist tradition: a 'mindfulness of spiritual friends' is recorded in a sutta in which the Buddha advises a lay disciple called Nandiya:

> *You should recollect lovely friends thus: a gain to me it is indeed! Well gotten indeed by me it is, that I have lovely friends, compassionate, desirous of my welfare, who encourage and exhort me. Thus, Nandiya, firmly fixed on lovely friends you should set up mindfulness in the inner self.*[97]

It seems that Anuruddha and his friends (whom we met in Chapter 2) were doing this practice. Each of them described his attitude to the others in words similar to some of those quoted above. If you aspire to be like them, you could therefore do no better than undertake this practice, at least occasionally, as a supplement to your main meditation practices. One can imagine various ways of doing it, such as mentally reciting the words quoted above while calling to mind some of your friends, thinking of those friends' good qualities, or reflecting on the ways in which their friendship has enriched your life.

Mind training, or *bhāvanā*, is not something that happens only on the meditation cushion. Some trace of it, at least, should continue in the midst of work, leisure, and social life. Otherwise, immersed in our daily preoccupations, we are likely to forget what happened in our meditation this morning, lose touch with spiritual ideals, and perhaps drift into unskilful mental states. You can't meditate all day, unless you live in a monastery (and most of us probably couldn't, even then). What you can do, though, is pause regularly in the course of the day to reconnect inwardly with your spiritual goal, and so gradually learn not to stray too far away from it. Eventually it will always be near the surface of your thoughts.

One helpful technique is to use 'triggers' – simple things like walking up or down stairs, or drinking – as reminders to turn your attention to your spiritual goal, and to check your mental state. Such methods are common to many forms of Buddhism. For example, if you are trying to develop mindfulness of the body, you might use such triggers as signals to relax and breathe more freely.

The same technique can be applied in the cultivation of kalyāṇa mitratā. You can learn to pause at intervals to call to mind one or more of your dearest spiritual friends.

The essence of all methods for developing feelings of spiritual friendship is to focus one's attention on the kalyāṇa, as it manifests in one's friends. Sceptics might question this strategy, arguing that by dwelling on the positive qualities of other people we falsely idealize them. But wise sympathy *is* objectivity, as far as other human beings are concerned. From the Buddhist viewpoint, the good qualities of human beings are those that contain the seeds of their future enlightenment. Their virtues are threads that connect them to reality, and in that sense are more real than their faults. Seeing human beings in this light, we can honestly acknowledge their weaknesses (and our own) without lingering over them unnecessarily. Friendship is the ideal context in which to awaken this insight.

The mindfulness of spiritual friends, including the cultivation of mettā and śraddhā for them, is the basic mental duty of friendship. Many obstacles stand in its way, but I want to discuss three major ones: cynicism, resentment, and the mind's dependence on the physical senses. The respective antidotes to these poisons are trust, forgiveness, and fidelity.

Trust: overcoming cynicism

A heart with no capacity to trust would hardly be human. To trust is to feel no doubt about someone's good intentions. When you trust someone fully, you lose any wavering uncertainty about that person's goodwill: you know that he or she is good, can be relied on to behave well towards you, and will always make the effort to understand you. The importance of trust in friendship is obvious.

Unfortunately, we inhabitants of anomic society are not always very good at trust. I have many spiritual friends both in India and in the West, and I notice that Westerners' capacity for trust usually moves within narrower limits, at least in the early stages of their spiritual life. No doubt other cultures have their own problems, but it may be helpful to us to recognize our reluctance to trust.

Part of the reason for it, I suppose, is the social atomization of modern society, which I discussed in Chapter 4. In addition, perhaps, our culture and education have deeply implanted in us the idea that fair appearances often mask a banal or sinister reality. We know from biology, for instance, that beneath the beauty of birdsong a ruthless territorial struggle rages; psychology suggests that the rational face of man masks a cauldron of instincts. At the same time, writers and thinkers have become highly skilled at debunking heroes and deconstructing ideals, but offer little to fill the void blown open by their analyses. All in all, our education and culture are adept at teaching us to be sceptical and critical (very valuable lessons, of course), but weak at developing our sense of the kalyāṇa, or our confidence that there is any such thing.

To that extent, we breathe an atmosphere of cynicism. I don't mean we are always exploiting people, or sneering at them. We are cynical in the specific sense that we habitually lean towards scepticism about the possibility of genuinely altruistic and noble motivation. Lacking much conviction in the kalyāṇa, thoughtful men and women tend to wonder and worry about what might be lurking under the surface of things: other people may seem friendly, but what if they really want to take something from us, materially or emotionally? Inevitably, the same anxiety afflicts the view we take of ourselves: many of us are troubled by thoughts that there might be something deeply wrong with us that we can't see.

True, Buddhism itself tells us that things are not what they appear to be. However, modern cynicism is very different from Buddhist insight. The Dharma says that one can discover reality by paying more careful attention to experience, whereas we fear that appearances may never give us a reliable clue to the truth.

Our cynicism can be a stumbling block to the development of spiritual friendship. I don't advocate gullibility – just a greater inclination to believe that what appears to be generosity, for example, may really be generosity, and not just an attempt to buy approval; that idealism may actually be idealism, not just repressed emotions building castles in the air. We need to learn once again to recognize the kalyāṇa and to put our confidence in it. Of course, we will sometimes be disappointed; but overall and in the long run the rewards will be greater than the letdowns.

Perhaps I need to enter a small caution. What I have said elsewhere about openness is also true of trust: it is progressive – a direction or a tendency, not something to be demanded in full, as a right, at the outset of a friendship. This is implicit in the Buddha's teaching that a person's good qualities can only be surely discerned by means of long, careful, and intelligent scrutiny.[98] We have to tread a wise middle way between being too slow to trust and too quick.

Clearly, there is a close link between trust and śraddhā – our ability to discern the kalyāṇa. The standard English translation of śraddhā is 'faith', which is of course a synonym for 'trust'. If we can't put trust in what is trustworthy, then our eye for the kalyāṇa must be clouded in some way, and we need to cleanse it. We can do this by cultivating śraddhā, and the Buddhist tradition offers us various methods of doing so. An important one is the use of ritual forms – such as bowing, chanting, and making offerings – to develop a love of the kalyāṇa as represented by images and symbols. Ritual practices are very powerful, but in today's culture not everyone feels entirely at home with them. Fortunately, there are other ways to develop śraddhā – through practising ethics more scrupulously, through confession, and through cultivating generosity.

As our śraddhā grows stronger, so does our capacity for friendship based upon it. Little by little, we learn to see the kalyāṇa in our friends more clearly, and to trust it more wholeheartedly.

Forgiveness: overcoming conflict and resentment

Even the sangha is not immune from conflict. One of the most thought-provoking stories in the scriptures describes the eruption of a serious dispute among a community of well-intentioned monks.

It seems that two learned bhikkhus at a place called Kosambi got into a disagreement about a minor point of discipline: whether an innocuous action one of them had committed – leaving a water vessel in the wrong place – did or did not technically infringe the monastic rules. However, the quarrel was aggravated by inept communication and tactless behaviour on both sides. The monk who was allegedly at fault (an expert in the Buddha's discourses) disputed the charge laid against him, and called his accuser (a specialist in disciplinary rules) a liar. Outraged by the insult, the latter contrived to get the discourse expert suspended, that is, excluded from participation in the communal life of the monks. But the discourse expert refused to accept the

187

suspension, and rallied his friends to support his cause. And so something that began as a personal quarrel spread, as the associates of each monk formed into two mutually hostile cliques, driving a wedge through the local monastic sangha and raising the threat of lasting schism.

Two features of the story offer food for thought. Firstly, the records show clearly that, far from being habitual troublemakers, both the disputants were 'desirous of training'. In other words, they were both sincerely going for refuge to the Three Jewels. Indeed, each was an experienced and respected practitioner, with a personal following of monks who regarded him as their teacher. Secondly, it seems that not even the intervention of the Buddha himself could calm the ill will stirred up between the two factions. The tale therefore bears troubling witness to the power of anger to disrupt relationships, even among people of goodwill and high ideals.

The Buddha's intervention was skilful enough to pacify anyone even slightly inclined to be pacified. Tactfully, and without taking sides, he went to visit each of the opposed groups in turn, and urged moderation. To the disciplinary expert and his friends, he explained that they should not suspend a monk whom they knew to be 'desirous of training' merely because that monk did not agree that he had broken the monastic rules. To the discourse expert and his allies, he pointed out that the wisest course in such a situation, rather than cause schism, was to set aside one's private judgement and patiently abide by that of one's peers, if they were sincerely going for refuge.

Clearly, the Buddha's strategy was not to arbitrate the case, but to show the monks the importance of harmony, and the means to restore it. In effect he said to them (and to us), 'If your sangha, despite its imperfections, is a genuine sangha (that is, if you considered it to be such when you were in a calm frame of mind, before the quarrel exploded) then surely it is more important to maintain harmony within it than to prove yourself right on a single disputed point.' This gentle, even-handed wisdom should have been enough to calm everyone down, but feelings had reached too high a pitch. Things got worse, and 'quarrels, brawls and disputes broke out in the midst of the Sangha'.

When the Buddha directly pleaded with the monks to put an end to harsh speech, they went so far as to dismiss him, under a show of courtesy, by asking him not to concern himself with the matter. Never one to force anything on anyone, the Buddha withdrew and went to visit Anuruddha and his friends.

Eventually, the quarrel at Kosambi was resolved, but not before seriously undermining the confidence of the local lay community, and causing a lot of trouble to the wider sangha. It must also have left the participants with quite a backlog of unwholesome karma to work through after they finally patched up the quarrel.[99]

Everybody has faults, and nobody can please us all the time. Sometimes, friends only begin to see one another's faults once the friendship has reached a certain degree of intimacy, when they let go of inhibitions and show their characters more fully. Because they know us well, friends are particularly well placed to hurt us. When they do, a sense of betrayal compounds the pain of our wounded feelings. We should therefore not be surprised when tension or disharmony suddenly intrudes on what seemed a thriving friendship. In fact, we would do best to look on it as a great spiritual opportunity: dealing with quarrels and resentment is one of the challenges that define the adventure of kalyāṇa mitratā.

Resentment is one of the greatest obstacles barring the way to enlightenment. From the Buddhist viewpoint, it is an unskilful emotion and is never 'justified'. As the *Dhammapada* movingly puts it,

> *Those who entertain such thoughts as 'He abused me, he beat me, he conquered me, he robbed me,' will not still their hatred.*

Those who do not entertain such thoughts as 'He abused me, he beat me, he conquered me, he robbed me,' will still their hatred.[100]

Spiritual friendship is the best school for learning to let go of resentment because it provides the most favourable conditions. The ideal of kalyāṇa mitratā, together with the methods of Buddhist mental training, the practice of confession, and the supportive context of the sangha (including more mature friends) all equip us, as nothing else can, to conquer negative emotions. If we cannot overcome resentment in these conditions, how will we ever overcome it? On the other hand, if we do succeed in overcoming resentment in the context of spiritual friendship, we will thereby create a stronghold against it in which we can gather strength to attack it in other areas of our life.

As preparation for this challenge, it is a good practice to examine oneself and discover what sorts of things tend to spark resentment. Is it to be teased? To be interrupted when speaking? Made to feel inferior by other people's knowledge? Do you sometimes feel exploited by somebody's slowness to bear their share of some mutual task, leaving too much to you? If you know what sort of thing makes you grudge, you can forestall resentment by foreseeing how it might arise in an approaching situation.

But however carefully we avoid the conditions that produce it, we sometimes have to rid ourselves of resentment that has actually arisen. This is not so difficult in cases where, on reflection, we come to accept that the fault was largely on our own side. However, it may be that a friend really has behaved badly towards us. On these occasions, the only way forward is to practise forgiveness. This is a difficult and profound spiritual practice, to which meditation and reflection may be indispensable aids.

In spiritual friendship, forgiveness may be gradual, but it can't be provisional. As the same faults in the same friend may well provoke us again, it is not good enough to 'suspend the sentence' and store up grievances under a show of patience.

Forgiveness therefore has to be independent of whether or not we feel that the friend has fully acknowledged his or her part in a quarrel, or adequately apologized for it. This is a tall order: nothing less than a letting go of some of the strongest emotions associated with one's ego. The effort therefore strikes directly at our sense of self, and so draws us closer to enlightenment. The capacity to forgive is essential to the spiritual life.

In another sense, though, it isn't such a big deal. When I say that forgiveness is essential, I am classing it as 'basic', not as 'advanced'. When we manage it, we shouldn't get too pleased with our own magnanimity. If practising forgiveness gives us a pleasant taste of martyrdom, we can wash that away by remembering that it is not our lonely, heroic duty: our friends will often have to forgive us, too.

Fidelity: overcoming dependence on the senses

The foundation for spiritual friendship is a shared love of the kalyāṇa. But what if this foundation shifts or crumbles? How should we respond if one of our spiritual friends ceases to share our spiritual path? In a word, the answer is with fidelity.

For example, a friend might lose interest in spiritual practice (while remaining a morally upright person) and become immersed in other concerns. This is a pity, but need not be the cause of bad feeling, or the end of the friendship. Although no longer wishing to live a spiritual life, such a person may still be well disposed towards his or her former spiritual friends, and in that case it is good to keep up the friendship, in the spirit of fidelity.

I try to regard the love of the kalyāṇa as something that, once acquired, cannot be discarded once and for all. We can think of it (borrowing an image from the *Lotus Sūtra*) as a jewel sewn into the lining of someone's coat: the wearer may be oblivious to it, but cannot lose it. If one keeps up a connection with a friend who has abandoned spiritual practice, one's own śraddhā may eventually rekindle the friend's. However, one's efforts to keep up the connection should not depend upon this hope, or on any ulterior motive, but simply on mettā and the desire to honour the friendship.

Occasionally, one may encounter more difficult situations. What if a friend not only turns away from the spiritual community, but also turns *against* it? And what if this hostile attitude is expressed in unethical actions? Such cases are rare, but they can occur and are very painful. Even in such an extremity, the ideal response is to do what we can to restore the friendship, and to influence the estranged friend for the good. If, in such a case, a point is reached where one feels that communication is too painful, or is drawing one into unethical behaviour or unwholesome mental states, it may then be necessary to limit or break off contact. Even then, one can remain open to restoring the connection if circumstances change for the better.

When friends betray us, that doesn't justify betraying them in return. We might discover, for example, that they have revealed our secrets, or slandered us. Nevertheless, we can avoid speaking badly of them, and even try to speak well (and think well) of them, as far as we can, remembering that they were once our friends. We can try to dwell on the positive memories of the friendship, which may span years or decades, rather than on the final (but perhaps much shorter) period of antagonism. Above all, we can go on cultivating mettā towards them. It is good not to write off someone who was once a friend. Everyone with whom we have made a connection of friendship remains a part of us, in some sense, throughout life.

The duty to honour a friendship, even when the friend does not, is one important aspect of fidelity. Another is behaving consistently towards friends – not blowing hot and cold according to one's mood.

Fidelity also means maintaining one's feelings for friends even when you are separated from them for a long time. The sutta called 'The Way to the Beyond' is thought to be one of the oldest Buddhist scriptures, because it is referred to in other suttas. It contains what is perhaps the most memorable expression in Buddhist literature of the idea of maintaining a spiritual friendship in spite of physical separation. At the end of the sutta, the aged brahmin Piṅgiya returns home after a life-transforming encounter with the Buddha, one in which much of the conversation has been conducted by the telepathic exchange of thoughts. Piṅgiya tells his former teacher Bāvarī that he has found the Buddha to be 'a universe of wisdom', and concludes, 'This man, brahmin Bāvarī, is the man I follow.'

Possibly jealous but certainly curious, Bāvarī asks, 'Why then don't you spend all your time, your every moment, with this man Gotama [the Buddha], this universe of wisdom?' Piṅgiya replies,

> There is no moment for me, however small, that is spent away from Gotama, from this universe of wisdom.... With constant and careful vigilance it is possible for me to see him with my mind as clearly as with my eyes, in night as well as day. And since I spend my nights revering him, there is not, to my mind, a single moment spent away from him.... Whichever way this universe of wisdom goes it draws me with it. Physically, I cannot move like that – my body is decaying, I am old and weak – but the driving power of purposeful thought propels me without break.[101]

The bond between Piṅgiya and the Buddha was 'vertical', but the underlying principle expressed here is applicable to all kinds of close spiritual friendship, whether vertical or horizontal. Piṅgiya's story reveals the essence of fidelity: that one can only be faithful to a friend if the friendship has taken root in one's inner being, and is no longer dependent on outward conditions. Our human bodies are in the *kāmaloka*, the world of the five physical senses. The spiritually immature mind is mired in the data supplied by those senses: we easily get caught up in what we presently see, hear, touch, smell, and taste. That is why, when we are not meditating (and even when we are) we so easily forget our spiritual goals. Likewise, when we are not actually with our friends, we may gossip about them, criticize them, or just forget them.

Maturity in spiritual friendship is marked by non-reliance on the physical presence of the friend. In friendship, as in other aspects of spiritual life, we must develop the capacity to live on the plane of mind, rather than that of material circumstance.

The Buddha and (to a lesser extent) Piṅgiya were remarkable individuals. They could form a lasting connection on the basis of a single meeting. Most friendships can only get going on the basis of a long initial period when the friends see a lot of each other. But if their friendship becomes deep, and if the friends have the necessary character of mind, it can be sustained later on, even through times when conditions permit little contact between them.

We should therefore frequently reflect that our connection with a friend is not something that exists only when he or she is around. If we can keep friends in mind with love and goodwill, then we remain in touch with them even when a vast distance intervenes. Of course, this capacity exists to some degree in many ordinary friendships. Yet it is really rather remarkable. It only makes sense if one assumes that a good friend is in some way present within one's own mind.

We all have a mental image of each of our friends. Piṅgiya's capacity to see the Buddha with his mind was just an extremely highly developed form of this faculty. By 'image' I don't mean just a sort of mental snapshot (or even a whole portrait gallery); the image may or may not present itself in visual terms. A more important part of it is the unique, indefinable imprint that a friend leaves on one's feelings.

There is something mysterious about these mental images. In a sense, the image *is* the friend. Obviously, I don't mean that one's mental image is identical with the person: there is always more to a human being than what one perceives, even in his or her presence. Yet ultimately we cannot distinguish our image of a person from the actual person, because the image is our only link to that actuality. It is what allows us, each time we meet our friend, to pick up the friendship where we left off, without first having to mentally revise the history of the relationship. The image is our bridge to the friend.

What is more, to be in touch with the image – to have it vividly in mind – is to be in touch with the friend. If two friends call each other to mind regularly (especially in meditation) during a long mutual absence, they are likely to find, on being reunited, that by some strange means their friendship has deepened, in spite of the preceding separation.

This may sound a little mystical, but for me it is a matter of experience. I know that I remain in contact with my most important friends, in their absence, at the level of imagination. If I think of them, they are with me, often as vividly as if they were physically there.

I also believe that our mental images can put us in contact with absent friends in a quite literal sense: our thoughts about people, if we have an affinity with them, reach out towards them and affect them. I suspect that this goes on all the time, although the examples that come to mind are too elusive to describe effectively. Nevertheless, I think anyone who has some aptitude for meditation can get a taste of what I mean – perhaps during silent retreats, for example. In such settings one sometimes discovers, after the event, that everyone has been thinking the same thing at the same time. Something similar can happen among close spiritual friends – a subtle interaction that may continue even when they are not in the same place.

For those with any knowledge of the Dharma, such experiences are no more than what one would expect. Many scriptures, such as Piṅgiya's story in 'The Way to the Beyond', offer instances of telepathic communication. This is consistent with the Buddhist teaching that living beings cannot be understood only in terms of their physical form. As humans, we have bodies in the *kāmaloka*, but our mental being stretches up into higher levels – levels that we awaken by spiritual practice. At these higher levels, the dichotomy between 'self' and 'non-self' becomes less fixed. Physically, my body is 'here' while my friend's is 'there', but on the mental plane space becomes subordinate to consciousness: thoughts and feelings fly instantly to their object, regardless of distance. They may be communicated without words, looks, or gestures. They may even be *shared* – in the sense that it is impossible to say whose thoughts or feelings they are, one's own or one's friend's. There can be a co-arising of consciousness, based on a close harmony between two minds, which nevertheless suffer no loss of individuality. When this happens, the exchange of self and other, which I discussed in Chapter 6, ceases to be just a moral endeavour or an abstract metaphysical insight, and becomes a living experience.

Indeed, the power of friendship may cross not only physical barriers and spaces, but even the boundary between life and death. The *Bardo Thödol* (known in English as *The Tibetan Book of the Dead*) suggests that we can communicate with the dead. If this is true, it would seem natural for the contact to be stronger if the dead person is one with whom we had a friendship during his or her lifetime.

The thought that friendship may continue after death leads logically to the thought that it may also continue into future lives. In Buddhist literature, this is one of the teachings implicit in the *Jātakas* – stories of the previous existences of the Buddha. In them, the bodhisattva (the Buddha-to-be) often appears in the company of the friends who, in his final life as Gotama, will become his most intimate disciples: Ānanda, Sāriputta, and Moggallāna. Following the leadership and example of the bodhisattva, they perform good deeds together, and accumulate the merit they will ultimately need for their breakthrough to enlightenment.

We don't have to take the *Jātaka* stories literally. In general they seem to have the character of fables. But the doctrine of rebirth itself is much more than a fable, and the *Jātakas* express, through the medium of fable, a basic Buddhist assumption: that friendship has its own karma. The links we create with friends in our present lifetime, if strong enough, will tend to bring us together with them in future lives. This idea helps us to look beyond the narrow horizons of our present identity, and see friendship as a road threading a much vaster landscape.

The practical lesson we can take from this is the importance of creating a spiritual community now, in this lifetime. Creating a spiritual community means – as I hope you agree, if you have followed me this far – developing actual spiritual friendships. If you contribute to the development of the spiritual community, you are much more likely, in your next rebirth, to find yourself among friends who will encourage and aid you in the spiritual life, and share that life with you.

It is possible that you are already in the midst of such a process. When, in your spiritual search, you find a spiritual community and gain spiritual friends, it may feel as if a passing ship has unexpectedly dropped anchor at the island where you have long been marooned – lonely and famished. The vessel's arrival might seem to you no more than a wonderful piece of good luck, but in reality it might be something more like a homecoming. Perhaps, in a forgotten existence, you actually helped to build the ship.

Appendix

Friendship With What is Lovely

In Chapter 3 I point out that, in the English-speaking world, certain translations have until recently obscured the fact that *kalyāṇa mittatā* (the Pali form of *kalyāṇa mitratā*) means spiritual friendship – i.e. a relationship between persons. For example, there is the Pali Text Society translation (now many decades old) of the *Saṃyutta Nikāya*. This collection of suttas includes the conversation in which the Buddha tells Ānanda that kalyāṇa mittatā is the whole of the spiritual life, but in that particular sutta (and some others) the PTS translation renders *kalyāṇa mittatā* as 'friendship with what is lovely'.

Bhikkhu Bodhi, the most recent translator of the *Saṃyutta Nikāya* into English, has pointed out that such translations erred in translating *kalyāṇamitto* by such phrases as 'a friend of righteousness', 'a friend of what is lovely', etc. These translations, he remarks, 'all rest on a misunderstanding of the grammatical form of the expression'.[102] He himself translates it as 'good friend', and *kalyāṇa mittatā* as 'good friendship', thus restoring the sense of a personal relationship, rather than some abstract affinity for goodness.

In the context of the *Meghiya Sutta*, translators seem to have agreed that *kalyāṇa mittatā* means 'friendship with good persons', presumably because the story only makes sense if the words are understood in that way. Also, the Pali commentary on the *Meghiya Sutta* (which forms part of the commentary on the *Udāna*, now available in an English translation by Peter Masefield) takes *kalyāṇa mittatā* to mean personal friendship, not an abstract 'friendship with what is lovely'.

Some people, while accepting that *kalyāṇa mittatā* means 'spiritual friendship' in the *Meghiya Sutta* (and in most other contexts), argue that, in the conversation with Ānanda, the Buddha meant the words to carry the special meaning of 'friendship with what is lovely'. If Bhikkhu Bodhi is right, grammar alone is enough to render this position untenable. However, further light is cast by the commentary to the *Meghiya Sutta*, which refers to the passage in the *Saṃyutta Nikāya* and clearly assumes that, in speaking to Ānanda, the Buddha used the words *kalyāṇa mittatā* in exactly the same sense he had used them in speaking to Meghiya, i.e. 'possession of a lovely friend'.[103] While we can't assume that the commentaries are infallible in the interpretation of the suttas, they do represent the traditional understanding.

The combined evidence of grammar and the commentarial tradition are perhaps enough to settle the question, but it may be worth making two further points.

Firstly, could the Buddha really have meant to tell Ānanda only that 'friendship with what is lovely is the whole of the spiritual life'? If so, his message seems oddly vague and inconsequential. Presumably by 'what is lovely' he must have meant the Dharma, because the Dharma is often said to be 'lovely' (*kalyāṇo*) in its beginning, its middle, and its end (i.e. in its entirety). But what might he have meant by 'friendship' with the Dharma? Presumably what in more natural English we would call 'an affinity for' it. Let's assume that an affinity can include, or at least lead to, actual practice of the Dharma. But why tell Ānanda that 'the practice of the Dharma is the whole of the spiritual life'? Ānanda, though not the wisest of disciples, surely knew at least that much already. The impersonal interpretation of kalyāṇa mitratā is unsatisfactory because it reduces the Buddha's words to a truism.

Secondly – and here perhaps we get to the bottom of the whole debate – the refusal to allow *kalyāṇa mitratā* its normal translation in certain texts (while granting it in most others) seems to rest not on any actual feature of the texts concerned but on the prior assumption that the Buddha simply *could not* have meant that spiritual friendship is the whole spiritual life, and therefore must have meant something else. But why assume that?

One reason that might be offered is the traditional concept of the *paccekabuddha* – the idea that there must be 'solitary Buddhas' who have become enlightened without guides or companions, and who dwell happily enlightened without proclaiming it or sharing their wisdom with others. But are there really such entities as paccekabuddhas? The category may be an artefact, produced by extrapolation from certain statements in the earliest strata of the scriptures (especially the Buddha's reminiscence that he hesitated before deciding to teach the Dharma, which seems to suggest that he *might* have chosen to remain silent permanently). Even if there really are such beings, paccekabuddhas arguably represent a very unsatisfactory model of the spiritual life, lacking the compassion that is usually understood as integral to wisdom.[104]

Apart from a belief in paccekabuddhas, is there any other reason to doubt that the Buddha said that spiritual friendship is the whole of the spiritual life? To those who identify the Dharma exclusively with certain of its principles or practices – such as meditation (a solitary activity) or the overcoming of unwholesome attachment – the idea of friendship as an all-encompassing spiritual theme is hard to accept. It may even seem a dangerous heresy! But as I have tried to show, the idea has real and important meaning, and entails no contradiction of any other principle of the Dharma – though it may require some re-visioning of the relation of those principles to one another.

Notes

1   *Saṃyutta Nikāya 45: Maggasaṃyutta*, in Bhikkhu Bodhi (trans.), *The Connected Discourses of the Buddha: A Translation of the Saṃyutta Nikāya*, Wisdom Publications, Boston 2000. p.1524

2   The Pali form is *kalyāṇa mittatā*. The rationale for my choice of Sanskrit here is stated in the preface.

3   T.W. Rhys Davids and William Stede, *Pali-English Dictionary*, Pali Text Society, London 1992.

4   The formula occurs, for instance, in the *Samaññaphala Sutta*. For a translation see e.g. Maurice Walshe (trans.), *The Long Discourses of the Buddha: A Translation of the Dīgha Nikāya*, Wisdom Publications, Boston 1995, p.99; or Bhikkhu Bodhi (trans.), *The Discourse on the Fruits of Recluseship: The Samaññaphala Sutta and its Commentaries*, Buddhist Publication Society, Kandy, Sri Lanka 1989. p.29.

5   The Pali word is *brahmacariya*, which literally means 'faring like a god'. In some contexts, it has the specific sense of 'celibacy'. In the present context, however, it means the whole way of life leading to enlightenment; hence 'spiritual life'.

6   Bhikkhu Bodhi (trans.), *Saṃyutta Nikāya*, op. cit., p.1524.

Notes

7   Ibid., p.1525.

8   Ibid., notes, pp.1891 and 1892.

9   Ibid., pp.180–1.

10   My account of the *Meghiya Sutta* is based on the translations in Peter Masefield (trans.), *The Udāna*, Pali Text Society, Oxford 1994, and John D. Ireland (trans.), *The Udāna and the Itivuttaka*, Buddhist Publication Society, Kandy, Sri Lanka 1997.

11   Peter Masefield (trans.), ibid., p.63. Ireland's alternative translation (in brackets) suggests that a plural meaning (friends) is possible.

12   The Pali reads '*Idha Meghiya bhikkhu kalyāṇamitto hoti kalyāṇasahāyo kalyāṇasampavaṅko*'. The three synonyms are a formula that recurs in all the texts quoted thus far.

13   The medieval commentary supports this interpretation. The *kalyāṇa mitra* should have the capacity to communicate the Dharma, but this is only one of a wider range of attractive spiritual qualities. It is also clear that there must be an emotional response to the kalyāṇa as embodied in the friend: the bhikkhu 'proceeds, by way of both mind and body, in a state that slopes, tends, inclines towards lovely individuals alone'. In addition, the commentary evidently understands spiritual friendship as implying constant companionship: 'Since he [the bhikkhu] is accompanied by (*saha ayati*), proceeds along with, the aforementioned lovely (*kalyāṇa*) individuals in all bodily postures, being never without them, he is "one with a lovely companion" (*kalyāṇasahāyo*).' All this suggests friendship rather than a formal, impersonal relationship. See Peter Masefield (trans.), *The Udāna Commentary*, Pali Text Society, Oxford 1995, vol.2, p.573.

14   Peter Masefield (trans.), *The Udāna*, op. cit., pp.64–5 (with Ireland's alternative translations of some terms).

15   The Pali form is *ottappa*. The rationale for my choice of Sanskrit here is stated in the preface.

16   For a discussion of shame (*hrī*) and 'respect for wise opinion' (*apatrāpya*) and their role in Buddhist psychology, see Sangharakshita, *Know Your Mind: The Psychological Dimension of Ethics in Buddhism*, Windhorse Publications, Birmingham 1998, pp.125–9.

17 The Pali term is *cetovivaranasappaya*. The commentary explains that such talk is beneficial for the development of *samatha* (tranquillity) and *vipassanā* (insight) in two possible ways. Firstly, it cultivates these states indirectly 'through setting at a distance the hindrances that conceal the heart'. (These 'hindrances', which include the sensual and malicious fantasies that Meghiya experienced in the mango grove, are the negative mental states that obstruct *samatha* and *vipassanā*.) Secondly, such talk directly promotes the growth of tranquillity and insight: 'since it is suited, of service, to opening up, or to making manifest, that same consciousness associated with samatha and vipassanā.' Peter Masefield (trans.), *The Udāna Commentary*, op. cit., vol.2, p.581.

18 See Sangharakshita, *Know Your Mind*, op. cit., pp.141–4.

19 E.M. Hare (trans.), *The Book of the Gradual Sayings (Aṅguttara Nikāya)*, vol.4, Pali Text Society, Oxford 1995, p.231. Here, the Buddha instructs his monks on how to reply to 'wanderers of other views' when asked by them about 'conditions that wing to the awakening'.

20 The rationale for my choice of Sanskrit here is stated in the preface.

21 *Dīghajānu Sutta, Aṅguttara Nikāya* 6.4. See Nyanaponika Thera and Bhikkhu Bodhi (trans.), *Numerical Discourses of the Buddha, An Anthology of Suttas from the Aṅguttara Nikāya*, Altamira Press, Oxford 1999, p.221.

22 *Vinaya Mahāvagga* 1.23–4, as quoted in Ñāṇamoli, *The Life of the Buddha*, Buddhist Publication Society, Kandy 1992, pp.71–3.

23 My account is based on Peter Masefield (trans.), *The Udāna*, op. cit., pp.68–70, and John D. Ireland (trans.), *The Udāna*, op. cit., pp.56–8.

24 The story of Anuruddha and his friends is found in the *Cūḷagosiṅga Sutta* ('the shorter discourse in Gosiṅga'). My account of it is based on Bhikkhu Ñāṇamoli and Bhikkhu Bodhi (trans.), *The Middle Length Discourses of the Buddha: A Translation of the Majjhima Nikāya*, Wisdom Publications, Boston 1995, pp.301–6.

25 ibid., p.302.

26 That is, the *Khaggavisāṇa Sutta*, found in the *Sutta-Nipāta*.

27   H. Saddhatissa (trans.), *The Sutta-Nipāta*, Curzon Press, London 1985, p.5.

28   Bhikkhu Bodhi (trans.), *Saṃyutta Nikāya*, op. cit., pp.1543 and 1579.

29   Maurice Walshe (trans.), *Dīgha Nikāya*, op. cit., pp.461–9.

30   Ibid., verses 15–26.

31   Ibid., verse 24.

32   Ibid., verse 33.

33   Ibid., verse 23.

34   Ibid., verse 31.

35   Ibid.

36   Ibid., verse 23.

37   E.M. Hare (trans.), *The Book of the Gradual Sayings (Aṅguttara Nikāya)*, vol.4, op. cit., p.18.

38   From the *Mahāparinibbāna Sutta*. See Maurice Walshe (trans.), *Dīgha Nikāya*, op. cit., p.234.

39   H.V. Guenther (trans.), 'Excerpts from the Gaṇḍavyūha Sūtra', in *Tibetan Buddhism in Western Perspective*, Dharma Publishing, California 1977, p.11.

40   Ibid., pp.13–14.

41   Ibid., p.15.

42   Thomas Cleary (trans.), *The Flower Ornament Scripture, A Translation of the Avataṃsaka Sūtra*, Shambhala Publications, Boston 1993, p.1174.

43   Ibid., p.1178.

44   Ibid., pp.1179–80.

45   D.J. Enright and David Rawlinson (eds.), *The Oxford Book of Friendship*, Oxford University Press, Oxford and New York 1991, p.72 (modernized).

46   See e.g. Ann Monsarrat, *An Uneasy Victorian: Thackeray the Man*, Cassell, London 1980.

47   D.J. Enright and David Rawlinson (eds.), *The Oxford Book of Friendship*, op. cit., p.112.

48   Sir Thomas Browne, *Religio Medici*, in *The Major Works*, ed. C.A. Patrides, Penguin, London 1977, pp.142–3 (modernized).

49   *The Unquiet Grave*, quoted in D.J. Enright and David Rawlinson (eds.), *The Oxford Book of Friendship*, op. cit., p.19.

50   *The International Encyclopaedia of the Social Sciences*, Macmillan and Free Press, 1968.

51   National Statistics Online (http://www.statistics.gov.uk), according to which, the 2001 census revealed that 'the proportion of households containing one adult aged 16 to 59 was 15%, which was no different from 2000 but represents a threefold increase since the General Household Survey began, from 5% in 1971.'

52   Ibid., 'Adults moving house each year: by tenure before and after move, 1991–1996.'

53   Eric Hobsbawm, *Age of Extremes*, Abacus, London 1995, p.334.

54   C.S. Lewis, *The Four Loves*, Fount, London 1977, p.56.

55   Ibid.

56   Stuart Miller, *Men and Friendship*, Gateway Books, London 1983, p.2.

57   *The Rambler*, 27 October 1750, quoted in D.J. Enright and David Rawlinson (eds.), *The Oxford Book of Friendship*, op. cit., p.10.

58   Sir Francis Bacon, 'Of Friendship', in *The Essays of Francis Bacon, Lord Verulam*. Various modern editions exist. My quotation is taken from the Everyman edition, published by J. M. Dent, London n.d., pp.80–1.

59   Ibid., p.83.

60   Maurice Walshe (trans.), *Dīgha Nikāya*, op. cit., p.462.

61   Aristotle, *Nichomachean Ethics*, trans. Terence Irwin, Hackett Publishing Company, Indianapolis and Cambridge 1985, viii.2 (p.209), viii.3 (pp.211ff.).

62   See ch.31: 'Aristotle's Ethics', in Frederick Copleston, S.J., *A History of Philosophy*, vol.1, Doubleday, 1993.

63   Aristotle, *Nichomachean Ethics*, op. cit., pp.212–3.

64   Ibid.

65   Imām al-Ghazālī, *The Duties of Brotherhood in Islam*, trans. Muhtar Holland, Islamic Foundation, Leicester 1975, p.21.

66   Aristotle, *Nichomachean Ethics*, op. cit. See Irwin's glossary note on 'Fine, beautiful, *kalos*' and the associated references to the text.

67 *Śraddhā* is the Sanskrit form. The Pali is *saddhā*. The rationale for my choice of Sanskrit here is stated in the preface.

68 sGam.po.pa (Gampopa), *The Jewel Ornament of Liberation*, Herbert V. Guenther (trans.), Rider & Co., London 1959, p.33.

69 Nyanaponika Thera and Hellmuth Hecker, *Great Disciples of the Buddha*, Wisdom Publications, Boston 1997, p.30.

70 For a fuller discussion of going for refuge, see chapter 4 of my *Sangharakshita: A New Voice in the Buddhist Tradition*, Windhorse Publications, Birmingham 1994.

71 Śāntideva, *The Bodhicaryāvatāra*, trans. Kate Crosby and Andrew Skilton, Windhorse Publications, Birmingham 2002, pp.130–3.

72 Ñāṇamoli and Bodhi (trans.), *Majjhima Nikāya*, op. cit., p.302. For my account of the story of Anuruddha and his friends, see above, Chapter 2.

73 Maurice Walshe (trans.), *Dīgha Nikāya*, op. cit., pp.465–8.

74 Aristotle, *Nichomachean Ethics*, op. cit., ix.9 (p.257).

75 See above, Chapter 3.

76 Maurice Walshe (trans.), *Dīgha Nikāya*, op. cit., pp.251–2.

77 From *Parerga and Paralipomena*, quoted in D.J. Enright and David Rawlinson (eds.), *The Oxford Book of Friendship*, op. cit., p.22.

78 The source of this quotation (and the preceding remarks) is Douglass Roby's introduction to Aelred of Rievaulx, *Spiritual Friendship*, trans. M.E. Laker, Cistercian Publications Inc., Kalamazoo, Michigan 1977.

79 Michel de Montaigne: 'On affectionate relationships' in *The Complete Essays*, trans. M.A. Screech, Penguin 1991.

80 Aristotle, *Nichomachean Ethics*, op. cit., viii.8 (p.222).

81 'The More Loving One', from *Collected Poems*, ed. Edward Mendelson, Faber, London 1976, p.445.

82 Bhikkhu Bodhi (trans.), *Saṃyutta Nikāya*, op. cit., pp.173–4. (The same discourse is found in the *Udāna*.)

83 For a fuller discussion of this topic, see my booklet *Roads to Freedom*, privately published.

84 This image is found, for example, in the Islamic *hadith* (an utterance of the Prophet) about spiritual friendship, quoted by al-Ghazālī: 'Two brothers are likened to a pair of hands, one of which washes the other.' (al-Ghazālī, *The Duties of Brotherhood in Islam*, op. cit., p.21). The expression 'one hand washes the other' is also proverbial in English (and perhaps in other languages).

85 Ibid., p.22.

86 Robert A.F. Thurman (trans.), *The Holy Teaching of Vimalakirti: A Mahāyāna Scripture*, Pennsylvania State University Press, University Park and London 1976, p.150.

87 Bhikkhu Bodhi (trans.), *Samaññaphala Sutta*, op. cit., p.30.

88 Ibid., p.50.

89 *Pāmojja* (Pali) or *prāmodya* (Sanskrit).

90 Bhikkhu Bodhi (trans.), *Samaññaphala Sutta*, op. cit., p.30.

91 *Kevaddha Sutta*. See Maurice Walshe (trans.), *Dīgha Nikāya*, op. cit., pp.178–9.

92 Mentioned in e.g. the *Lakkhana Sutta*. See ibid., p.457.

93 Bhikkhu Bodhi (trans.), *Samaññaphala Sutta*, op. cit., p.30.

94 In his teaching to Mahāpajāpatī at *Aṅguttara Nikāya* 8.53. For a translation see e.g. Nyanaponika Thera and Bhikkhu Bodhi (trans.), *Numerical Discourses of the Buddha*, op.cit., p.220.

95 Bhikkhu Bodhi (trans.), *Samaññaphala Sutta*, op. cit., p.30.

96 Maurice Walshe (trans.), *Dīgha Nikāya*, op. cit., p.265.

97 F.L. Woodward (trans.), *The Book of the Gradual Sayings (Aṅguttara Nikāya)*, vol.5, Pali Text Society, Oxford 1996, p.215.

98 See Bhikkhu Bodhi (trans.), *Saṃyutta Nikāya*, op. cit., pp.173–4. I quote the passage in Chapter 10, above.

99 I have taken the story from Ñāṇamoli, *The Life of the Buddha*, Buddhist Publication Society, Kandy 1992, ch.8.

100 Sangharakshita (trans.), *Dhammapada* verses 3–4, Windhorse Publications, Birmingham 2001.

101 H. Saddhatissa (trans.), *The Sutta-Nipāta*, Curzon Press 1985, verses 1140–4.

102 Bhikkhu Bodhi (trans.), *Saṃyutta Nikāya*, op. cit., p.1890 (n.6).

103   Peter Masefield (trans.), *The Udāna Commentary*, op. cit., vol.2, p.574.

104   Sangharakshita makes this point more fully, and adds that even the
       Theravādin Abhidhamma seems to acknowledge it. See Sangha-
       rakshita, *The Three Jewels*, Windhorse Publications, Birmingham
       1998, p.142.

Index

211

Index